Beyond Pandemic
A Rebirth of Collective Consciousness

Michael Winger has contributed an interesting selection of inspirational stories highlighting the centre and heart of his book *Beyond Pandemic: A Rebirth of Collective Consciousness*. To these he has added provocative questions for reflection and discussion, many with roots in the world of science, that make reading this book an adventure in itself. I congratulate all who intend to embark on this global journey.

Peo Akerdahl, Retired Professor, University of Gävle, Sweden

As a reader who is not a Bahá'í, or not-yet Bahá'í, I enjoyed this captivating book. It sends a strong message about the way we should change our mindset and look at the world, not only focusing on our personal prosperity, but being concerned equally for the collective prosperity of all. Michael shares not only his life's experience, but also provides insights from science and others' stories that make the mystical more approachable. Many of us will become better persons after reading this book!

Marin Škufca, CEO, Liburnia Maritime Agency

. . . inspired from the very beginning. Michael really pulled it all together. It's everything I'd ever hoped to read in connection with science, religion and the Bahá'í Faith... I'm convinced this book will reach many searching hearts as it has my own.

Julie McKinney, Costa Rica

Utterly engaging. Michael has taken the science behind belief and made it not only palatable for simpler minds, like my own, but confirming for those who knew it all along. I think this book will meet an important need within the young by giving them new tools . . .

Andi Seals, artist and author

Beyond Pandemic
A Rebirth of Collective Consciousness

by

Michael Winger

GEORGE RONALD
OXFORD

George Ronald Publisher
Oxford
www.grbooks.com

A catalogue record for this book is
available from the British Library

ISBN 978-0-85398-638-6

Cover photograph: Michael Winger
Cover design: Steiner Graphics

Contents

Foreword

by Jason Neidrich[1]

Today is a time for deep reflection on what our reality is now and what it must be going forward. The world is in the midst of potentially catastrophic trials and tribulations. The Covid-19 global pandemic creates a stress that none of us in the present generation has had to face and, in some respects, nor have earlier generations. Not only has the global tumult caused stress in the physical realm, but the spirit of humanity, challenged daily by increasing trauma, requires constant reflection on who we are and who we collectively want to be.

Twenty-five years ago, I met Michael Winger and felt his palpable exuberance for finding disparate details in the far edges of science and technology trends. I enjoyed his weaving of those mysteries back into inspirations on how to grow in knowing and loving our Creator. That fire was as contagious then as this work is now!

Just as those early conversations were never meant to simply entertain, this book is not for the armchair quarterback. No, my friend. This book is a call to action. These stories have an undertow of, 'So, what are you going to do differently with this information and inspiration?'

Were you expecting a gentle read to accompany you on a picnic? Sincerely and unapologetically – choose another author.

My life has been engaged in discovery, invention and innovation since that time twenty-five years ago. The process of discovery and invention begins with a thought, an observation, a reflection or a stimulus that causes the mind to say, 'Hmm, I wonder.' And then, 'Why not?!'

The idea, like a grain of sand in the oyster, begins to irritate and fester. A slow penetrating annoyance enters into every thought and act and curiosity cannot be dismissed, until it demands action. One turns and twists the idea and then begins a process of search and belief that through the thicket and briars suggests that a potential path exists for a solution.

When the potential pathway is discovered the real work of proving begins. Along the way, one recognizes the efficacy of a trajectory and begins to beat the path to solution. This recognition demands more research, experimentation and proof. Once the path is confirmed, the process of fulfilment is then trodden to completion, refinement and classification.

The path to physical discovery reflects the path to spiritual discovery and the processes are similar. As in scientific discovery, one begins with a belief that there is an unknowable Essence and then one discovers a path to spirituality. That recognition also requires study, experimentation and proof. Then one must tread that path to confirmation and certitude.

This book identifies the four essential questions that every seeker must answer on his or her spiritual quest. Michael weaves a web of scientific discovery and mystical exploration through the magic of storytelling. He illustrates, illuminates, coaches and inspires the reader to forge a discipline and gain the equipment that will enable the fulfilment of the quest. The actors in these stories become companions of the reader and bring to life the struggles and rewards of the adventure.

This book intends you to make your own stories. Think of the stories in this book as broad shoulders for you, the active reader and open-hearted seeker, to stand upon to see your own path and hold your birds-eye view on your spiritual journey.

I hope you will want to keep this book close at hand as a traveller's guide during this spiritual odyssey. I wish you all the best on your transformational journey and hope you feel that Michael comes out of these pages and sits in the room with you, lovingly, supportively, and expectantly, asking you, 'What's next?'

Acknowledgements

It is my hope that readers of this book will enjoy it as much as I have enjoyed writing it. Remembering and gathering the stories that accompany the text inspired the writing.

We live in a time of great transitions and transformations, collectively and individually. Even before the Covid-19 pandemic took an unsuspecting world by surprise in early 2020, I had become increasingly concerned that the upheavals in society and the decline of decency in the political realm had not only polarized humanity, but was contributing to a general sense of hopelessness among the peoples of the world.

As humanity drifts further into a morass of senselessness and looks to 'celebrities' for its heroes, or conversely to a veneration of militarism, the need for a pathway to a spiritual renewal becomes daily more necessary and evident. Thus the purpose of this book.

Most people of my generation (+65) are too deeply affected by entrenched ways of thinking and by blind imitation. The generations that followed mine, who occupy leadership positions and hold current responsibilities in their hands, are often overwhelmed by the needs of the hour. It is my hope, therefore, that the youth of this day may read this book and find a different and more advanced dialogue than those that are current in the news, a dialogue that will facilitate the needs of future leaders.

Since physically entering into the mature years of life, I long to experience this maturity in my being as well, but writing this book and gathering the stories for it has given me a youthful vibrancy.

I look to the youth of the present generation with great admiration and expectancy. To all my peers in my own generation and the next, I say: tune your eyes, hearts and minds to these vibrant and idealistic young people and assist them to take up the mantle that we, who have struggled to be builders of a new world, have shouldered. They will take it to distances that we could never imagine.

Many people influence our lives. Some give us joy and some give us tests. To all who have crossed my path, I thank you for helping me to grow.

I would like to thank my beloved wife, Helena Vasco, for her unwavering love and support while I ignored the world to write this. Her excitement in listening to each story and chapter, and the insights she provided, gave me the encouragement and energy to press onward when I just wanted to go play pool.

Thank you to my dear friends Jason Neidrich, Ramin Farahani. Julie McKinney, Andi Seals, Marin Škufca and Peo Akerdahl who provided invaluable reviews, comments, insights and suggestions that gave me the confidence to finish this. I am forever indebted to you. It is always a blessing to have good friends who will tell you lovingly that you are missing the point or that you are deep in some woodland that no one else occupies. And sometimes, that you are doing just fine.

And finally to George Ronald Publisher, whose confidence, patience and most professional editing has assisted in the drawing out from my heart with clarity what I have wanted to say, and furthered the completion of this book.

I look forward to hearing from you, the reader of *Beyond Pandemic*, and hope that the book inspires you to, as Bahá'u'lláh writes, *When the swords flash, go forward! When the shafts fly, press onward!*

Introduction

The global pandemic that changed the world in early 2020, and the subsequent challenges that are emerging as a result, propel us to consider what is beyond this moment and in what ways will we arise to create a global collective consciousness. What is latent within humanity to bring about the transformation required?

In Jewish tradition, on Passover, four questions are asked during the Seder, the traditional commemoration of the Jewish people leaving their bondage from Pharaoh. The Mah Nishtanah (the four questions) asks:

- Why is this night different from all other nights?
- What unique power does the night of Passover hold that it can inspire even the most distant soul and touch even the most stubborn sceptic?
- What must we do on this night that will change our perspective?
- What will open our spiritual eyes and ignite our souls?

Today, in a similar fashion we ask these big four questions:

- What is the first duty of a human being in this day?
- What is the first obligation of a Bahá'í?
- What must be the all-compelling concern of our lives?
- What is the one thing that will make our spiritual endeavours successful?

On the path, or rather the spiritual odyssey of life, these questions will beg an assortment of evolving answers that challenge our thinking about their significance to us in our daily lives over time. The purpose of this book is to provide the traveller on his or her spiritual path with a guide to develop the discipline necessary for the journey. At this time of world peril, we look for answers and directions to take that will assist humanity as a whole, and ourselves as individuals, to reach safe shores and calm waters. A message from the Universal House of Justice, the world governing body of the Bahá'í Faith, written in March 2020 to the Bahá'ís of the world, makes clear the role the Bahá'ís are called upon to play at this time:

> At a time of another crisis, 'Abdu'l-Bahá offered these words of counsel: 'In a day such as this, when the tempests of trials and tribulations have encompassed the world, and fear and trembling have agitated the planet, ye must rise above the horizon of firmness and steadfastness with illumined faces and radiant brows in such wise that, God willing, the gloom of fear and consternation may be entirely obliterated, and the light of assurance may dawn above the manifest horizon and shine resplendently.' The world stands more and more in need of the hope and the strength of spirit that faith imparts . . . you have of course long been occupied with the work of nurturing within groups of souls precisely the attributes that are required at this time: unity and fellow feeling, knowledge and understanding, a spirit of collective worship and common endeavour.[1]

I believe that among the most provocative and profound resources for the journey before us are observation and discovery within the natural and scientific world. The harmony of science and religion has been a challenge and occupation of most of history since the dawning of the intellectual age (the time of Plato and Socrates). In the 19th century, science entered revolutionary fields causing humankind to contemplate concepts never before imagined. Mankind leaped from the world of Isaac Newton and his mechanistic order into the world of Einstein and Planck's quantum uncertainty disorder. Ilya Prigogine and Isabelle Stengers, in their groundbreaking book, *Order Out of Chaos*, attempt to reconcile these two schools of thought and describe a world of non-equilibrium and chaos creating a world of order. They identified this reconciliation as dissipative structures.

Ilya Prigogine (b. 1917) was both a chemist and a physicist. His research on dissipative structures found that 'these structures, when far from equilibrium, can transform small-scale irregularities into large-scale patterns'. The Bahá'í Faith, in Prigogine's and Stengers' world, provides a dissipative structure out of which a new order will emerge. For over one hundred and seventy years, the Bahá'í community worldwide has moved in an opposite direction to the generality of mankind. Its small-scale irregularity continues its march to a new order.

Another dissipative structure in the organic world is the development of the butterfly. Inside the chrysalis spun by the caterpillar, it is unable to move, and dissolves into organic goop that feeds its transformation. Imaginal cells, a term coined by Dutch biologist Jan Swammerdam, which had been dormant in the caterpillar and are completely different from those of the caterpillar, begin a process of creating a new form and structure. Imaginal cells can also be described as a dissipative structure within the chrysalis.

At first these imaginal cells – the seeds of future potential, which contain the blueprint of a flying creature – operate independently as single-cell organisms. They are regarded as threats and are attacked by the caterpillar's immune system. But they persist, multiply, and connect with each other. The imaginal cells form clusters and clumps, begin resonating at the same frequency and pass information back and forth until they hit a tipping point. They then begin acting not as discrete individual cells, but as a multi-cell organism – and a butterfly is born.

If the caterpillar could think as a human and imagine its future, it could never imagine a new world as a butterfly. It would perceive a utopian existence based on its experience as a caterpillar. Perhaps it would imagine fields rich in foods without any predators. Wonderful weather that allows it to thrive among other caterpillars. It could never imagine the beautiful colours waiting to manifest themselves, never conceive of flying over vast areas and assisting in the pollination of flowers and plants. Such is the character of organic growth. It differs dramatically from evolutionary growth in that the former is consumed in the emergence of the new.

If the caterpillar were to interrupt the decay and destruction necessary to fuel the emergence of the new organism, it would retard the very future it is destined to become. And, interestingly, if one were to assist the butterfly to emerge from the cocoon during its arduous struggle, it would never fly. The difficulties encountered in the struggle to leave the cocoon are necessary to build the strength for the wings to function and lift the body into the air.

This provides an analogy for the growth and influence of the Bahá'í Faith. Its institute process and core activities have emerged into a multi-cell organism and expand the world-circling imaginal cells which are here to transform the 'goop' of society. As the emergence of the new order from God expands, the old order is consumed in decay and destruction and fuels new growth and transformation.

Human spiritual renewal, like its butterfly twin, moves from a caterpillar state, whose main function is to serve itself and survive, to the state of the butterfly, whose function is to serve the world in its role of pollination. The main difference is that the imaginal cells in the caterpillar are innate parts of the organism from its beginning and activated automatically.

In human society, the imaginal cells are dormant until recognition of the Manifestation of the Day activates them by man's own will. In the words of Shoghi Effendi:

> All we can reasonably venture to attempt is to strive to obtain a glimpse of the first streaks of the promised Dawn that must, in the fullness of time, chase away the gloom that has encircled humanity.[2]

The Bahá'í community worldwide reflects a similar dissipative structure in the global community. The imaginal cells of its future are forged and embedded in those believers who recognize its source and follow its guidance. Shoghi Effendi writes:

> The Community of the Most Great Name, the leaven that must leaven the lump, the chosen remnant that must survive the rolling up of the old, discredited, tottering Order and assist in the unfoldment of a new one in its stead, is standing ready, alert, clear – visioned, and resolute . . .[3]

The task of the Bahá'í community is organic change, not evolutionary. It is not the goal of the Bahá'ís to simply improve the existing society or to help it evolve to a more mature place. Although we must be compassionate, caring and contributing citizens of the world, the Bahá'í vision expresses a new world order, not an improvement of the old. While mankind as a whole is going through an evolution into its maturity, the society in which mankind exists is undergoing an organic change, a complete transformation.

Bahá'u'lláh in the Kitáb-i-Aqdas, His Most Holy Book, unfurls the process that we are engaged in accomplishing:

> The world's equilibrium hath been upset through the vibrating influence of this most great, this new World Order.

> Mankind's ordered life hath been revolutionized through the agency of this unique, this wondrous System – the like of which mortal eyes have never witnessed.[4]

Once we embrace the recognition of Bahá'u'lláh, we begin to transform into the imaginal cells that will enable the entity's existence and begin to grow a new race of men. Again referring to the butterfly in the caterpillar state, the caterpillar serves only itself. It eats, breathes, and moves about primarily to just survive. However, when the organic change or transformation occurs, the butterfly begins to serve the world in its function of pollination. This 'new race of insect', if you will, moves into an advanced state of service to all of creation. It moves from selfishness to selflessness.

Central to this transformation for the Bahá'í is the recognition of oneness – one God, one religion unfurled over millennia, one human race. The forces of the past resist, recoil and attack the emerging entity and will continue to do so until a tipping point has occurred. One could say that this tipping point is fast approaching.

This book will explore this dissipative structure and identify the questions an individual must answer to survive and thrive during this tumultuous period. Let us explore the concept of eternity and its relationship to phenomenal existence – first, to identify the four big questions to answer and then, the four essential practices to employ while investigating this quest.

Once the 'big four' questions have been explored, the four essential practices will be identified that will lead to a life-sustaining, life-thriving and life-transforming discipline that will enable one to travel through this revolutionizing and turbulent period of global upheaval. This discipline will lead to a life of calm in the midst of the storm, confidence in the face of tribulation, and provide purpose to life in the chaos of transformation.

It is my hope that the reader will appreciate the efficacy of this framework and take actions to assist in the creation of a world whose arrival mankind has for millennia contemplated and prayed for. Humankind is in the throes of an organic change – a change that tears asunder the past order and, while consuming the putrefaction of its decay, will emerge from the chrysalis and chaos of transformation into an order of unimaginable splendour and wonder. It is our choice collectively and individually whether we are to be submerged into the decay, or choose to join the yeast of emergence into the new. As the Universal House of Justice has written, in April 2020:

> Two emerging realities have prompted us to address these words to you. The first reality is the growing consciousness around the world of the looming and appalling dangers carried by the coronavirus pandemic. In many countries, despite valiant and determined collective efforts to avert disaster, the situation is already grave, creating tragedies for families and individuals and plunging whole societies into crisis. Waves of suffering and sorrow are breaking over one place after another, and will weaken different nations, at different moments, in different ways.[5]

The path we choose will be conditioned on the recognition of who we are, of what is our purpose in this existence, what is our relationship to our very creation, and what must we do to build the strength and capacity to take the actions necessary to fulfil the goals of our choices.

To the youth of this generation, take heart! Recognize the moment we are living in, make these essential choices for your lives and arise knowing that the future of the world depends on you and that you have the capacity to move the world. So, mount up, grab the reins and lead the charge!

I

Accident or Creative Will?

Acknowledgement of belief

If we were to deny all that is not accessible to the senses, then we would be forced to deny realities which undoubtedly exist. For example, the ether is not sensible, although its reality can be proven. The power of gravity is not sensible, although its existence is likewise undeniable. Whence do we affirm their existence? From their signs. For instance, this light consists in the vibrations of the ether, and from these vibrations we infer its existence.

'Abdu'l-Bahá[1]

The existence of the unseen has been the quest of humans for millennia. One might say: if you cannot see it, touch it, feel it, taste it or hear it then it must not exist. Yet modern science has attacked this thinking for several centuries with increasing persistence, confidence and fervour. The entire field of physics increasingly suggests the existence of that which cannot be perceived by the senses. In this age of light, humanity finally accepts the reality of the unseen in many arenas.

One of the final (and continuing) frontiers in the pursuit of the unseen is the understanding of our very existence. Are we consciously created or are we just a part of an accidental series of events beginning with a Big Bang and evolving over billions of years? If we are created, is it in a scheme that is completely prescriptive with the tiniest exercise of the human will and each moment programmed by the micromanagement of an all-pervasive and judgemental Will? Or has that creative Will just rolled the dice and sits in a lounge chair to observe what emerges?

Herein lies the difficulty for the individual who struggles with the distinction between those who believe in a Creator but suffocate in doctrine, the agnostic who fades into the shadow of leaving the question unanswered, or the atheist who denies the creative force completely. There is, of course, the possibility, as well, of the existence of randomness created by a Creative Will, thus allowing for the exercise of individual will within some undefined parameters. As Vahid Houston Ranjbar, a physicist at the United States Brookhaven National Laboratory, writes:

> the word 'spirit' is commonly looked on at worst as a product of old superstitious thought, or at best a vague expression of emotion or feeling. Yet if we look beyond the historical baggage of this word, we can find words in contemporary physics which basically appear to carry the same essential meaning.
>
> . . . For many years now physicists have lived with this new idea of a non-material field. Yet if we're honest, this idea doesn't seem so different from the ancient religious idea of a non-material spirit. We may not like the word due to the connotations it carries, but at its basic level the ideas are exactly the same. A field is a non-physical thing which permeates space – exactly the definition of a spirit.[2]

A friend told a story of his university days where once he mentioned to a roommate that he was a member of the Bahá'í Faith. His roommate replied, 'I don't believe any of that. I'm an atheist!'

The friend replied, 'So am I.'

'How can that be?', his roommate inquired.

'Well, I don't believe in that same God that you don't believe in.'

'Then, what is it that you believe?' he asked, curious.

'Well, let's begin a dialogue then,' the friend answered.

For those who accept the accidental model of existence, there is a paradox. The accidentalist requires proofs and scientific confirmation. So should the believer. But absolute proofs are elusive. Of course, most of science is based on theoretical models that provide sufficient evidence to make the theory workable. Einstein's difficulty with the unified model of physics was with the anomalies of the theory of gravity in the sub-atomic world. We know that gravity exists, the evidence is sufficient. But it is still, from a scientific point of view, a theory.

One of the fundamental maxims in science is that there are no exact duplicates in all of the universe. There are no water molecules that are exact duplicates of each other. Thus, the paradox: If all of creation is accidental, then the theory of probability would require a duplicate. Probability theory suggests that within an infinite space there exists the probability that a certain number of identical occurrences will manifest. Therefore, in the infinity of creation, a number of duplicate occurrences would manifest if all of creation were accidental or unintentional.

For the doctrinal believer, one must abdicate at least a bit, if not more, of the individual investigation of truth to a set of doctrines that other men have prescribed and are not explicit in their Holy Texts. For many, this is a comfortable pathway and provides sufficient solace.

The agnostic, for the most part, is satisfied living on the fence and experiencing life as it presents itself. Whether there is life after death, whether there is a Primal Will, do not present an important part of the day-to-day struggles of life.

These distinctions prompt the story of the scientist who spoke with God. God was sitting in heaven one day when a scientist said to Him, 'God, we don't need you anymore. Science has finally figured out a way to create life out of nothing – in other words, we can now do what you did in the beginning.'

'Oh, is that so? Explain . . .', replies God. '

'Well,' says the scientist, 'we can take dirt and form it into the likeness of you and breathe life into it, thus creating man.'

'That's very interesting . . . show Me.'

So the scientist bends down to the earth and starts to mold the soil into the shape of a man.

'No, no, no . . .' interrupts God, 'Get your own dirt.'

Albert Einstein is often reported to have said: 'To know that what is impenetrable to us really exists, manifesting itself as the highest wisdom and the most radiant beauty, which our dull faculties can comprehend only in their primitive forms – this knowledge, this feeling, is at the centre of true religiousness.'

The seeker who accepts and acknowledges the existence of a Creator begins the attempt to understand and become comfortable with the idea of belief. One of the fundamental principles of the Bahá'í teachings is the harmony of science and religion. This demands the recognition of the oneness of all of creation – the seen and the unseen as one. The laws governing each are one – applied differently.

For example, believers in any faith community accept love as a central law or principle. Some say, 'God is love.' Yet the Creator cannot be so limited in definition, as the Creator created love. Love in a spiritual sense is unseen. It is not defined by any sensory confirmation. It transcends the senses. Although telephone time between lovers can certainly be measured.

Love in the physical world can be understood by the law of attraction. Hydrogen and oxygen are subject to the physical attributes of love and bind together to create the water molecule. There is a physical attraction and a mysterious binding catalysed by heat. Why some particles bind and others do not provides some mystery to the equation. Not all oxygen particles and hydrogen particles combine or we would need gills to breathe. Yet, bind they do and the observer sees the law of attraction, the physical expression of love, become manifest.

An explosion in the pursuit and dissemination of knowledge began in the mid-1800s and speeds up daily. One of the main drivers in this acceleration derives from the change from classical single-disciplinary approaches to inter-disciplinary teams of collaborative investigation. Scientific discovery expands in both the micro and macro arenas as we more clearly recognize the unlimited boundaries in both directions. To quote from an article by Alan Leshner in *Science* magazine:

> We are learning another important lesson: that no field stands alone. Progress in any one domain is absolutely dependent on progress in many other disciplines. For example, these applications of brain imaging technology depend on simultaneous progress in chemistry and physics. Similarly, progress in the information sciences is a prerequisite for dealing with the tremendous quantities of new data being generated in fields such as genomics, with its huge sequence arrays, or astronomy, with databanks generated from modern radiotelescopes.
>
> In a related way, we are now seeing more and more truly interdisciplinary science. Thirty years ago, one might have called *Science* a multidisciplinary journal; after all, it has long published papers from many different fields. But now many of our papers involve teams of scientists from many specialties, bringing diverse expertise to bear in an integrated rather than merely parallel way. The fact that this interdisciplinarity characterizes so much of today's most exciting work may portend the gradual demise of single-discipline science.[3]

The more science advances, the more the unseen world is unveiled. The more the unseen is unveiled, the more science recognizes that the boundaries of our knowledge are limitless. As we attempt to approach infinity, infinity moves further from us, it seems.

'Abdu'l-Bahá in the book *Some Answered Questions* (1908) spoke of 'ether'. He mentioned that light 'consists in vibrations of the ether' (see the quotation at the beginning of this chapter). At the time, science was much more immature and the 'educated' saw His comments as merely symbolic. However, in 1964, physicist Peter Higgs suggested a similar concept based on his research in particle theory. In 2012, his 1964 discovery of the Higgs Field was confirmed at the Fermi Laboratory in Switzerland and the *Higgs boson* was observed. François Englert and Peter W. Higgs were granted the Nobel Prize in Physics for their discovery.

The Higgs boson (crudely coined 'The God Particle' by fellow physicist and Nobel Laureate Leon Lederman) was the last particle of the 'Standard Model' of physics to be discovered. It occupies a unique and essential place in that theory, and its discovery validated our understanding of how fundamental particles can have mass. Higgs' research was a stage in the unending process of the pursuit of science and its illumination of the unseen.

When one acknowledges that what has been created requires a creator, that something does not magically spring from nothing, one begins a unique lifelong exploration. We can never be absolute in our pursuit of knowledge because exploration necessarily brings forth new knowledge. Our limitations depend on observation, exploration, accepted theories, evidence and a degree of confirmation. Reality is infinitively small and infinitely large.

Ten years ago, with the use of the most advanced telescopes, it was determined that the known universe contained around 300 billion galaxies consisting of about 300 billion stars each. Our Milky Way galaxy is one of the smallest galaxies observed. Today, with continued advancement, astronomers now recognize that the known universe has over 1.4 trillion galaxies. To put this into some small context, imagine a room that is 5 metres long by 5 metres wide by 3 metres tall. Now imagine an atom, invisible to the eye or to a microscope. This atom represents the earth in our own galaxy. And we are part of 1.4

trillion galaxies, most of which are considerably larger than the Milky Way!

Here is another way to contemplate stellar size. The Voyager 2 probe was launched in 1977. It is the longest running and farthest travelling object sent into space from earth. In November 2018 it entered an area of our solar system called interstellar space where our sun's solar wind and magnetic field gives way to other galactic forces. It is still well within our solar system though. According to calculations of the Jet Propulsion Laboratory, it will take another 30,000 years for Voyager 2 to exit our solar system if it keeps going. And this was accomplished by an on-board computer that is 200,000 times less powerful than today's average smart phone!

The pursuit of knowledge will never end or be complete. Limitation will be conditioned on currency – that is, what we know at present. Today, our current knowledge of physics suggests that approaching the speed of light is the fastest anything can travel. This limitation is based on current understanding and application of physics. Time travel is impossible in the physics of our world as we know it. Since the universe is constantly expanding, so is time and the outer fringes of time is always now. Anything else exists only in our imagination and dreams. And it will remain so until our knowledge, theories and exploration fundamentally change what we currently understand and recognize.

Interestingly though, *quantum entanglement* suggests that all particles in the universe are connected and communicate at speeds faster than light. This is an area of quantum theory that Einstein called 'spooky action at a distance'. He observed and recorded the mathematics that suggested this possibility. At the CERN Laboratory on the Swiss/French border, it was physically confirmed in 1997 when a particle was split in half and the two halves were separated by 14 kilometres. Each responded identically and instantly to the same stimulus given only to one half!

The renowned scientist and astronomer Carl Sagan is widely reported to have said, 'If we ever reach the point where we think we thoroughly understand who we are and where we came from, we will have failed.'

In the next chapter we will explore belief and recognition. The remainder of this book is dedicated to the process of living in a world of evolving recognition of the Creative Will and our role in the process of bringing forward an ever-advancing civilization. We are invited to individually and collectively bring universal salvation to the unfoldment of a future that we can only dimly imagine. Bahá'u'lláh writes:

> The birds of men's hearts, however high they soar, can never hope to attain the heights of His unknowable Essence. It is He Who hath called into being the whole of creation, Who hath caused every created thing to spring forth at His behest.[4]

Further considerations

God grant that, with a penetrating vision, thou mayest perceive, in all things, the sign of the revelation of Him Who is the Ancient King, and recognize how exalted and sanctified from the whole creation is that most holy and sacred Being. This, in truth, is the very root and essence of belief in the unity and singleness of God. 'God was alone; there was none else besides Him.' He, now, is what He hath ever been. There is none other God but Him, the One, the Incomparable, the Almighty, the Most Exalted, the Most Great.

Bahá'u'lláh[5]

All blessings are divine in origin, but none can be compared with this power of intellectual investigation and research, which is an eternal gift producing fruits of unending delight. Man is ever partaking of these fruits. All other blessings are temporary; this is an everlasting possession.

'Abdu'l-Bahá[6]

Exercises

Over the next two weeks, engage in a meaningful conversation with a believer in God (any religion), an agnostic, and an atheist. Without trying in the least to change his/her mind, to convince him/her of anything, or to teach him/her anything, seek to find the answers to the following:

1. What are 5 reasons that they believe the way they do?

2. How did they come by this belief?

3. In what ways do they think their beliefs will help society in a positive way?

4. What strategies would you employ to follow up on this initial conversation to further your relationship with this individual?

5. What did you learn?

2

The Created Spirit

Belief to recognition: What is our first duty?

The first duty prescribed by God for His servants is the recognition of Him Who is the Dayspring of His Revelation and the Fountain of His laws, Who representeth the Godhead in both the Kingdom of His Cause and the world of creation.

Bahá'u'lláh[1]

One can only believe in a Creator, as He is an Unknowable Essence. Any concept, description, imagination or thought would be far from the reality of One Who is beyond our reality. However, we can approach that Unknowable Essence through the observation of what is created and manifested.

Recognition of God is impossible. However, we can recognize His Manifestation. We can learn about God's Will through the teachings of the Manifestation of God. We can observe what is offered to us. It is the primary duty of the rational mind to seek, contemplate and acknowledge its Creator and His Manifestation.

Throughout the millennia, the Creator has sent innumerable divine teachers to mankind. These Manifestations of God each bring forward an unfolding understanding of reality tuned to the exigencies of the time. For most of humanity, this unfoldment is missed, as individuals and clergy cling to the former teachers and reject the following ones. Followers of Abraham reject Moses who then reject Christ, who then reject Muhammad, or followers of Krishna who reject Buddha and so on. It is like the student in love with his or her teacher in a former grade who rejects the teachers that follow to the next levels or grades.

For the Bahá'í, his or her first duty is the recognition of the Manifestation of God for this day and the acknowledgement of one creation, one Creator, one humanity, one unfolding religion.

Michio Kaku, one of the preeminent physicists of today and founder of the String Theory in physics, writes an interesting observation:

String theory and M-theory are based on the simple and elegant idea that the bewildering variety of subatomic particles making up the universe are similar to the notes that one can play on a violin string, or on a membrane such as a drum head. (These are no ordinary strings and membranes; they exist in ten- and eleven-dimensional hyperspace.)

Traditionally, physicists viewed electrons as being point particles, which were infinitesimally small. This meant physicists had to introduce a different point particle for each of the hundreds of subatomic particles they found, which was very confusing. But according to string theory, if we had a Super-microscope that could peer into the heart of an electron, we would see that it was not a point particle at all but a tiny vibrating string. It only appeared to be a point particle because our instruments were too crude.

This tiny string, in turn, vibrates at different frequencies and resonances. If we were to pluck this vibrating string, it would change mode and become another subatomic particle, such as a quark. Pluck it again, and it turns into a neutrino. In this way, we can explain the blizzard of subatomic particles as nothing but different musical notes of the string. We can now replace the hundreds of subatomic particles seen in the laboratory with a single object, the string.

In this new vocabulary, the laws of physics, carefully

constructed after thousands of years of experimentation, are nothing but the laws of harmony one can write down for strings and membranes. The laws of chemistry are the melodies that one can play on these strings. The universe is a symphony of the strings. And the 'Mind of God,' which Einstein wrote eloquently about, is cosmic music resonating throughout hyperspace. Which raises another question: If the universe is a symphony of strings, then is there a composer?[2]

In Kaku's vocabulary, if there is a composer, how does He communicate His Will to us? One's belief accepts that which is unknowable, but definition and certainty are impossible. However, through the recognition of the Primal Will's Manifestation, we can begin to approach certitude by testing the Creative Word through its efficacy in our lives. We can move from belief to recognition to certitude.

We are given clear instructions for the testing and confirmation that leads to certitude. We learn to pray. We carefully imbed the Creative Word of the Manifestation into our minds and vocabulary. We read the Creative Word in both the morning and the evening of each day. We begin a life of service to others and perform deeds that reflect the Creative Word. As we embark on this behaviour and build a daily routine, we reflect on our lives and begin to notice changes in our outlook, our happiness, our contentment and our hopefulness. It is not a prescription that reduces the stress and difficulties of life, but a transformation in our response to life's vicissitudes.

Prayer begins with the humility that recognizes that we are weak and in need of a higher power. It focuses our minds on a greater Force to assist us in our lives. Prayer gives us a focal point into an eternal existence for which we have been created. It enables us to see that we are a soul having a physical experience, not a physical being having a spiritual experience. 'Abdu'l-Bahá explains:

The whole physical creation is perishable. These material bodies are composed of atoms; when these atoms begin to separate decomposition sets in, then comes what we call death. This composition of atoms, which constitutes the body or mortal element of any created being, is temporary. When the power of attraction, which holds these atoms together, is withdrawn, the body, as such, ceases to exist.

With the soul it is different. The soul is not a combination of elements, it is not composed of many atoms, it is of one indivisible substance and therefore eternal. It is entirely out of the order of the physical creation; it is immortal!

Scientific philosophy has demonstrated that a simple element ('simple' meaning 'not composed') is indestructible, eternal. The soul, not being a composition of elements, is, in character, as a simple element, and therefore cannot cease to exist . . .

Consider the aim of creation: is it possible that all is created to evolve and develop through countless ages with this small goal in view – a few years of a man's life on earth? Is it not unthinkable that this should be the final aim of existence?[3]

Scientific theory today acknowledges the concept of multi-dimensions and multi-universes. However, in theory, only simple elements – those not composed – can move between multi-dimensions and multi-universes. Hence, when the soul separates from the physical association to the body, it travels to another, eternal existence or universe or dimension.

It is through our prayers, acts of service and good deeds followed by careful and sustained reflection in our lives that we see the effects of the recognition of God's Manifestation. Quite simply, prayer is conversation with the Creator. And, during prayer, the focus on the Manifestation allows us to connect to that which is recognizable rather than that which is unknowable. On one hand, prayer is an act of humility that requests assistance beyond our own capabilities. On the other, it is the expression of gratitude for having been created and the assistance we receive. It is in our obedience to the Laws of Creation that we transform from a materially-focused being into a spiritually-focused being.

A member of the Bahá'í Faith recounted the following story:

A group of us were sitting in the living room in the home of the Hand of the Cause of God, William Sears. He said to us that if we want to be happy and serve the Faith, we need to acquire attributes of God. The best way to do this is to choose one attribute and with all your heart, mind and actions strive to put that attribute into practice. As you do this, other attributes of God will also become manifest in you. And, the best way to acquire that attribute would be to take one Hidden Word and make it your own. Strive to make that Hidden Word the focus of your life and manifest it the best you can. You will see that as you do that, all the attributes of God will slowly enter into you.

One of Bahá'u'lláh's titles is the 'Sun of Reality'. Since this Being manifests the Creator to us, it also expresses the reality of creation, both in the seen world and the unseen worlds. The Manifestation of God reveals to us the Will of the Creator and the laws that govern all of creation, both the seen and the unseen. 'Abdu'l-Bahá wrote:

The Graces of the Kingdom of Abhá are the rays of the Sun of Reality. It illumines the earth and heaven, makes the star a shining moon, turns the speck into a huge mountain, bestows strength to the weak, gives everlasting healing to the sick, grants heavenly treasures to the poor, confirms the oppressed ones to everlasting glory and turns the people of darkness to those of light.[4]

As we move from belief to recognition to certitude, we begin to act with increasing faith. Faith is 'conscious knowledge acted upon' as my dear friend Nathan Rutstein used to express it. It is action based in principle, responsive to our beliefs, and in accordance with our recognition of the Manifestation of God for today.

An old Cherokee Native American told his grandson, 'Son, there is a battle of two wolves inside us all. One is Evil. It is anger, jealousy, greed, resentment, lies and ego. The other is Good. It is joy, peace, love, hope, humility, kindness, empathy and truth.'

The boy thought about it and asked, 'Grandfather, which wolf wins?'

The old man quietly replied, 'The one we feed.'

A letter written on behalf of Shoghi Effendi says:

The Teachings of Bahá'u'lláh are so great, and deal with so many aspects of both the inner life of man and his communal life, that it takes years to really plumb them to the depths. He has brought spiritual food for the soul of the individual, to help each one to find himself and become a finer and better developed personality; and also He has brought the laws and principles needed to enable all men to live in harmony together in a great, united world.[5]

Further considerations

Be thankful to God for having enabled you to recognize His Cause. Whoever has received this blessing must, prior to his acceptance, have performed some deed which, though he himself was unaware of its character, was ordained by God as a means whereby he has been guided to find and embrace the Truth . . . We cherish the hope that you, who have attained to this light, will exert your utmost to banish the darkness of superstition and unbelief from the midst of the people. May your deeds proclaim your faith and enable you to lead the erring into the paths of eternal salvation.

Bahá'u'lláh[6]

Deign, O my God, I implore Thee, by Thy Self and by them, to accept, through Thy grace and Thy loving-kindness, the works we have performed, however much they fall short of the loftiness of Thy state and the sublimity of Thy station, O Thou Who art most dear to the hearts that long for Thee, and the Healer of the souls that have recognized Thee! Rain down, therefore, upon us from the heaven of Thy mercy and the clouds of Thy gracious providence that which will cleanse us from the faintest trace of evil and corrupt desires, and will draw us nearer unto Him Who is the Manifestation of Thy most exalted and all-glorious Self. Thou art, verily, the Lord of this world and of the next, and art powerful to do all things.

Bahá'u'lláh[7]

Exercises

1. What are five characteristics of belief?

2. What are five characteristics of recognition?

3. In your life's experience, describe something that demonstrates the difference between belief and recognition.

4. Memorize a Hidden Word and meditate on it each day for two weeks. After the two weeks, reflect on the Hidden Word and describe its effect on you. Can you describe any changes in yourself? In your language? In your outlook? In your actions?

3

Purposeful Growth

Knowledge, significance and understanding:
What is our first obligation?

*To strive to obtain a more adequate understanding of the sig-
nificance of Bahá'u'lláh's stupendous Revelation must, it is my
unalterable conviction, remain the first obligation and the object
of the constant endeavor of each one of its loyal adherents. An
exact and thorough comprehension of so vast a system, so sublime
a revelation, so sacred a trust, is for obvious reasons beyond the
reach and ken of our finite minds. We can, however, and it is our
bounden duty to seek to derive fresh inspiration and added sustenance as we labor for the propagation of His Faith through a
clearer apprehension of the truths it enshrines and the principles
on which it is based.*

Shoghi Effendi[1]

There is a battle going on. It spreads across all areas of our
lives. Its frontline – the war between the forces of darkness
and light. The battleground is for the soul of man. Its target
– the hearts of humanity. The calls to battle are between individual salvation and collective salvation. The former seduces
the individual to greed, power, self-indulgence, personal gain,
the focus on self-awareness and growth, and personal well-
being. The latter desires the betterment of the world, the
upliftment of everyone by the sacrifice of self to the collective
good, and the recognition that the betterment of all brings the

well-being of individuals. Shoghi Effendi, the Guardian of the Bahá'í Faith, writes:

> The more we search for ourselves, the less likely we are to find ourselves; and the more we search for God, and to serve our fellow-men, the more profoundly will we become acquainted with ourselves, and the more inwardly assured. This is one of the great spiritual laws of life. [2]

The distinction between individual salvation and collective salvation lies in the strategies, tactics and results. For individual salvation, the strategy is to focus on the individual, its tactics are personal growth and the results would be the benefit to society. If I am good and everyone else is good then society benefits. This is dependent on every individual striving to be good. What is the motivation? What will propel the individual to strive to be good? For collective salvation, the strategy is the betterment of the world, its tactics are service to humanity and the result is the upliftment of the individual. When the focus is on a collective, all participants uplift each other for a common purpose. The choice between these two is not an easy one, but necessary. To put it in a Star Trek quote, Commander Spock, in one episode, says, 'Logic clearly dictates that the needs of the many outweigh the needs of the few.' Captain Kirk answers, 'Or the one.'

In 1944, Shoghi Effendi sent this cable to the Bahá'ís in North America: 'First century of Bahá'í era drawing to a close. Humanity entering outer fringes most perilous stage its existence.'[3] The two world wars broke the outer shell of humanity's societies and facilitated the entrance into this perilous stage whose outer fringes we had only entered in 1944. Our immediate future is very dark, leading to that promised dawn of a glorious age that we can only dimly imagine.

To return to the butterfly analogy in the Introduction to this book, we spin the cocoon of the future out of the destruction of the past. Now is the time for the destruction and consumption of the old, so that the organic change can mature. This process will take much time, involve much hardship, create great chaos and confusion, and ultimately result in the birth of a new life that the past cannot predict, the conscious cannot envision, and the dreamers cannot imagine. As 'Abdu'l-Bahá explained:

> When a cycle comes to a close, a new one is inaugurated, and the previous cycle, on account of the momentous events which transpire, vanishes so entirely from memory as to leave behind no record or trace. Thus, as you are aware, we have no record of twenty thousand years ago, even though life on this earth is very ancient – not one or two hundred thousand, or even one or two million years old: it is ancient indeed, and the records and traces of ancient times have been entirely obliterated.
>
> Each of the Manifestations of God has likewise a cycle wherein His religion and His law are in full force and effect. When His cycle is ended through the advent of a new Manifestation, a new cycle begins. Thus, cycles are inaugurated, concluded, and renewed, until a universal cycle is completed in the world of existence and momentous events transpire which efface every record and trace of the past . . .[4]

The cells of the caterpillar cannot assist in the growth of the butterfly except to be consumed in the process and provide sustenance. If the imaginal cell of the butterfly were to turn its gaze on the decay and destruction of the caterpillar, it would retard, postpone or even destroy the development of the butterfly – the very purpose it was created for. In the same way, the Bahá'ís are the imaginal cells of Bahá'u'lláh's New World Order. Bahá'u'lláh describes the believers as the yeast that must leaven the world. If the believers focus on the destruction of the world, they too could retard or postpone the development of the New World Order.

For the individual, the imperative is to strive to obtain an understanding of the significance of this period in history, the forces that have led to this time, the roadmap to humanity's future, the role of the individual and the collective efforts necessary to survive and thrive in this turbulent period of transition. We can *derive fresh inspiration and added sustenance* in this quest for understanding as we labour for mankind's collective salvation. Understanding in this day requires not only diligent study, but actions and deeds that confirm that which we study.

Humanity has evolved through the stages of its development from infancy to childhood to youth and now is in its most dangerous period of late adolescence. In infancy, laws for the protection of the child are by necessity restrictive and almost entirely within the family unit. As the child grows, social laws enlarge the family to its neighbours and the restrictions are more moderate. The child is taught how to love others outside the family unit.

In the period of youth, many ideals emerge and extended relationships begin farther afield from the family. Not all activities are family-centred. Adolescence begins the twilight between the capacity of the adult and the shifting emotions from child to adult in rhythmic swings. The adolescent is now in the most dangerous period – unfettered by the restrictions of the family, exploring his/her own individuality, exercising the full power of an adult while struggling with the emotional cacophony between child, youth and adult. The adolescent has the power of self-destruction on one hand and the idealism of social awareness and engagement on the other. It is a scary time, certainly for the parents and society, but also for the adolescent as he or she searches for footing without direct family support.

Humanity is now in the late stages of adolescence. It will pass through this period and mature into an adult fully capable of contributing to society at large, and will leave its past turbulence behind. Some think that since we have always had war, greed, poverty and suffering, this will forever be the condition of humanity. Would we look upon our sons and daughters in the same light as they go through the stages of life? No, we see a future for them that will be filled with light and hope. We understand that they will mature through their tests and difficulties and emerge as successful contributors to society. The members of the Bahá'í community worldwide see the same for humanity.

Every person must choose between personal salvation or collective salvation. It is a defining decision of our lives. The impact of our decisions is often not initially apparent. The changes in our lives can often be subtle, painful and slow. It is for this reason that Bahá'u'lláh quotes the saying, 'One hour's reflection is preferable to seventy years pious worship.'⁵ Other effects of our decisions may not occur in our lifetime or many years into the future. The Creative Will of God has endowed every soul with the capacity to recognize His Manifestation and arise to serve the betterment of the world. We are also endowed with a free will to choose to do so or not.

On a business trip to Chicago once it was my joy to be there on fireside night at the home of the Khadems. The Hand of the Cause Mr Khadem and his dear wife Javidukht hosted a fireside gathering every Tuesday evening. When they were travelling, someone else would come to their home to host.

Mr Khadem always attended the gathering only after the speaker was finished so as not to interrupt the speaker as the Bahá'í friends would want to hear from him. On this evening, however, Mr Khadem was there at the beginning. He opened the meeting by saying, 'I want to be here tonight and introduce our speaker. He has a wonderful story about himself that he would not share with you due to his humility. But I want you to know this story.'

Mr Tim Farrand was a long-time pioneer to El Salvador and was visiting Chicago. Tim came from a very distinguished military family whose members had served in the armed forces in every war since the Revolutionary War. He became a Bahá'í prior to the Korean War. When he was drafted, he applied and received non-combatant status, as was the practice for Bahá'ís. Bahá'ís served, but were given conscientious objector status so as not to be in a combat position that would force them to kill another human being. He became a military nurse.

Tim's father was furious with him because of his non-combatant status and felt he had betrayed the history of the family. He disowned Tim. This was a source of great sadness for Tim, but his faith did not diminish.

Tim served meritoriously in Korea and came home a decorated soldier. Upon his return, in 1955, he had another year of service to perform and was stationed at a military hospital in Colorado. While there, President Eisenhower was visiting the area and suffered a heart attack. Tim was assigned to attend to the President. Over the time the President was there, they developed a friendly relationship that went beyond just Tim's professional attendance to the President.

At this time, the Bahá'ís in Iran were undergoing severe persecution; there was great destruction to the Bahá'í community and many believers were killed. There seemed to be no end in sight, as many nations of the world condemned the acts to no avail.

When it was time for the President to return to Washington DC, before leaving he called for Tim to come to his room. He said to Tim that he appreciated his service to him personally and wanted to know if there was anything that he could do for him. Tim said, 'No, Mr President. It was my honour to serve you.' And he began to leave the room. But as Tim came to the door, he turned to the President and said, 'There is one thing you could do, sir. I am a Bahá'í. My fellow Bahá'ís in Iran are being persecuted terribly and if there is anything you could do on their behalf that would be wonderful.' And he left.

The President brought the full weight of his Presidency to

bear as he admonished the Shah of Iran to intervene to stop the persecution of the Bahá'ís. Soon the horror abated. As well, the President, unaware of Tim's beleaguered relationship with his father, wrote a letter to Tim's father. In the letter he praised Tim's service to the country and told his father that no soldier on the field of battle had done as great a service to his country than what Tim had done in his service to his President. Of course, Tim's father reconciled with his son and was proud of him.

A postscript to this story: several years ago I was on a trip to Costa Rica and was a speaker at a gathering. I felt inspired to tell the story of Tim. Towards the end of the story, I noticed a woman sitting there with tears streaming down her face. She came to me after the talk and said, 'Thank you for that story. Tim was my father and although I knew that he was President Eisenhower's nurse once, I had never heard the story.'

As we study the Writings of the Faith, or writings from scholars in the sciences, humanities and other arenas, our striving should be on the significance of our reading to the betterment of the world. The significance we derive should be tested in action, reflection and refinement. This process unfolds to us the efficacy of the truths and principles that we desire to obtain and the progress we make, little by little. It brings us confirmation, strength and commitment to proceed forward. Bahá'u'lláh writes:

> These journeys have no visible ending in this temporal world, but the detached wayfarer – should invisible confirmation descend upon him and the Guardian of the Cause assist him – may traverse these seven stages in seven steps, nay rather in seven breaths, nay even in a single breath, should God will and desire it. This is 'a token of His grace vouchsafed unto whomsoever He pleaseth.'[6]

Further considerations

Know ye not why We created you all from the same dust? That no one should exalt himself over the other. Ponder at all times in your hearts how ye were created. Since We have created you all from one same substance it is incumbent on you to be even as one soul, to walk with the same feet, eat with the same mouth and dwell in the same land, that from your inmost being, by your deeds and actions, the signs of oneness and the essence of detachment may be made manifest. Such is My counsel to you, O concourse of light! Heed ye this counsel that ye may obtain the fruit of holiness from the tree of wondrous glory.

Bahá'u'lláh[7]

Fellowship and love amongst the believers. The divine friends must be attracted to and enamored of each other and ever be ready and willing to sacrifice their own lives for each other. Should one soul from amongst the believers meet another, it must be as though a thirsty one with parched lips has reached to the fountain of the water of life, or a lover has met his true beloved. For one of the greatest divine wisdoms regarding the appearance of the holy Manifestations is this: The souls may come to know each other and become intimate with each other; the power of the love of God may make all of them the waves of one sea, the flowers of one rose garden, and the stars of one heaven. This is the wisdom for the appearance of the holy Manifestations!

'Abdu'l-Bahá[8]

While the work of teaching inevitably goes first, to pursue it alone without consolidation would leave the community unprepared to receive the masses who must sooner or later respond to the life-giving message of the Cause . . . Consolidation must comprise not only the establishment of Bahá'í administrative institutions, but a true deepening in the fundamental verities of the Cause and in its spiritual principles, understanding of its prime purpose in the establishment of the unity of mankind, instruction in its standards of behaviour in all aspects of private and public life, in the particular practice of Bahá'í life in such things as daily prayer, education of children, observance of the laws of Bahá'í marriage, abstention from politics, the obligation to contribute to the Fund, the importance of the Nineteen Day Feast and opportunity to acquire a sound knowledge of the present-day practice of Bahá'í administration.

The Universal House of Justice[9]

Exercises

Let there be no mistake. The principle of the Oneness of Mankind – the pivot round which all the teachings of Bahá'u'lláh revolve is no mere outburst of ignorant emotionalism or an expression of vague and pious hope. Its appeal is not to be merely identified with a reawakening of the spirit of brotherhood and good-will among men, nor does it aim solely at the fostering of harmonious cooperation among individual peoples and nations. Its implications are deeper, its claims greater than any which the Prophets of old were allowed to advance. Its message is applicable not only to the individual, but concerns itself primarily with the nature of those essential relationships that must bind all the states and nations as members of one human family. It does not constitute merely the enunciation of an ideal, but stands inseparably associated with an institution adequate to embody its truth, demonstrate its validity, and perpetuate its influence. It implies an organic change in the structure of present-day society, a change such as the world has not yet experienced.   *Shoghi Effendi*[10]

1. In what ways does this quotation from the writings of the Guardian relate to the transformation of the caterpillar into the butterfly?

2. What is the institution adequate to embody its truth?

3. List five 'imaginal cells' latent in the world today that will remain in the organic change in present-day society

4. Over the next two weeks, engage in a hopeful manner in a meaningful conversation with someone about the organic change in society.

5. In what ways did this meaningful conversation influence you? Upon reflection, what did you learn?

4

The Act of Spirit

Many roads, many choices:

What is our all-pervading concern?

Upon every participator in this concerted effort . . . rests the spiritual obligation to make of the mandate of teaching, so vitally binding upon all, the all-pervading concern of his life. In his daily activities and contacts, in all his journeys, whether for business or otherwise, on his holidays and outings, and on any mission he may be called upon to undertake, every bearer of the Message of Bahá'u'lláh should consider it not only an obligation but a privilege to scatter far and wide the seeds of His Faith, and to rest content in the abiding knowledge that whatever be the immediate response to that Message, and however inadequate the vehicle that conveyed it, the power of its Author will, as He sees fit, enable those seeds to germinate, and in circumstances which no one can foresee enrich the harvest which the labor of His followers will gather.

Shoghi Effendi[1]

Sharing our recognition of Bahá'u'lláh with others is an act of love. It is the confirmation of the transformation in our lives to serve the betterment of the world. There are many avenues and methods that we can employ in this work of the heart. The material world demands quantifiable and visible results. The materialist likes to count things and measure growth. Although these attributes are important, for spiritual development, process and principle will contribute to a greater advancement in the long run.

In the field of teaching, measures of advancement are more important than metrics of performance. Both are important, but metrics count things and identify quantifiable outputs. Measures identify advancement and determine outcomes from process. For the success of teaching, process and measures of effectiveness are more important initially and over time will contribute to quantifiable results.

For example, the number of new believers in an area is a metric that is easily identified. However, the measure of a community's health for fostering active involvement in community growth is much more difficult to determine. For long-term growth of a community, it would be better to identify the measures of a community's health to insure continuous growth rather than merely the number of new believers. To measure both would be preferable.

To understand the process of teaching, we again turn to science. In chemistry, there are two types of bonding that occur at the molecular level – ionic and covalent bonds.

Covalent bonds have a definite and predictable shape and have low melting and boiling points. They can be easily broken into primary structure as the atoms are close by to share the electrons. These are mostly gaseous, and even a slight negative or positive charge at opposite ends of a covalent bond gives them molecular polarity.

Ionic bonds normally form crystalline compounds and have higher melting points and boiling points compared to covalent compounds. They require much more *energy* than covalent bonds to break the bond between them. In a sense, the bond we form with our Creator is an ionic bond. We are a weaker being that requires a stronger Being and the bond once formed is extremely strong and very difficult to break. The bonds we form with one another are covalent bonds in that the bonds between equals require constant attention to remain connected. A covalent bond can easily be broken from estrangement, distance, backbiting and gossip, or misunderstandings. The Universal House of Justice has written:

> The House of Justice hopes that all the friends will remember that the ultimate aim in life of every soul should be to attain spiritual excellence – to win the good pleasure of God. The true spiritual station of any soul is known only to God. It is quite a different thing from the ranks and stations that men and women occupy in the various sectors of society. Whoever has his eyes fixed on the goal of attaining the good pleasure of God will accept with joy and radiant acquiescence whatever work or station is assigned to him in the Cause of God, and will rejoice to serve Him under all conditions.[2]

In our teaching efforts, the time and effort required to form and maintain the bonds of friendship (similar to the covalent bond) are significant and must be nurtured through love, accompaniment, patience and persistence.

There are two types of teaching efforts currently employed – personal and collective. Personal teaching is required of every Bahá'í. The methods are not prescribed, but the principles of how to teach are exhaustive in the Writings of the Faith. Collective teaching is also a benefit to growth and provides a great learning laboratory for enabling success in personal teaching and rapid growth in communities, especially among youth.

Our involvement in the teaching work is as Shoghi Effendi expresses, vitally binding upon all. This means that our spiritual advancement depends on our teaching the Cause. He does not prescribe the methods of teaching, but provides clear principles that we should follow in both our personal and collective efforts.

Whatever method or process we engage in to teach the Faith, it is important to remember these words of the Guardian,

Let him not be content until he has infused into his spiritual child so deep a longing as to impel him to arise independently, in his turn, and devote his energies to the quickening of other souls, and the upholding of the laws and principles laid down by his newly-adopted Faith.[3]

Ultimately the goal of teaching is the upliftment of the individual and the betterment of the world. In the words of 'Abdu'l-Bahá:

Every imperfect soul is self-centred and thinketh only of his own good. But as his thoughts expand a little he will begin to think of the welfare and comfort of his family. If his ideas still more widen, his concern will be the felicity of his fellow citizens; and if still they widen, he will be thinking of the glory of his land and of his race. But when ideas and views reach the utmost degree of expansion and attain the stage of perfection, then will he be interested in the exaltation of humankind. He will then be the well-wisher of all men and the seeker of the weal and prosperity of all lands. This is indicative of perfection.[4]

Amatu'l-Bahá Rúḥíyyih Khánum shared one of her memories that she was once in a fireside with a group of Persian and British pioneers. One of the seekers was a black man who was sitting there and was listening carefully. Suddenly the door opened and the daughter of one of the English pioneers came in with her milk bottle in hand. She looked at the audience and went directly to the black man and made it to his lap and managed to sit there. She smiled at him, and kissed him. She started to drink her milk from the bottle and then fell asleep. One of the Persian ladies tried to reach the baby to grab her from the man's lap, but Rúḥíyyih Khánum told her, in Persian, 'Let her be, she is teaching the Faith in her own way.'

After the meeting, the man approached Khánum and told

her that he would like to be like her and go wherever she went to teach the Faith. <u>Kh</u>ánum looked at him and asked if he was a Bahá'í? And he said yes, he was.

Rúḥíyyih <u>Kh</u>ánum was astonished and asked, 'Since when? How and why?' He said, 'Since an hour ago when that little girl went to me, kissed me, and sat on my lap and slept there with great calm. Since that moment I thought to myself that she had a different and brilliant education where there was no hint of racism. Her parents must have had no prejudice in educating her like that. And then I said to myself, this is the Faith I must grasp. That is why I am a Bahá'í now.'

Bahá'u'lláh writes:

Do thou ponder these momentous happenings in thy heart, so that thou mayest apprehend the greatness of this Revelation, and perceive its stupendous glory. Then shall the spirit of faith, through the grace of the Merciful, be breathed into thy being, and thou shalt be established and abide upon the seat of certitude.[5]

Further considerations

Say: To assist Me is to teach My Cause. This is a theme with which whole Tablets are laden. This is the changeless commandment of God, eternal in the past, eternal in the future. Comprehend this, O ye men of insight.

Bahá'u'lláh[6]

O ye servants of the Blessed Beauty! . . . It is clear that in this day, confirmations from the unseen world are encompassing all those who deliver the divine Message. Should the work of teaching lapse, these confirmations would be entirely cut off, since it is impossible for the loved ones of God to receive assistance unless they teach.

'Abdu'l-Bahá[7]

My dear and precious co-worker:
You should exercise your judgement and tact in delivering the message. You should make an effort to understand the character and mind of the seeker before you speak to him on the Cause. I will pray that you may be inspired and guided to follow the path of moderation and may become an exemplary herald of His message in that far-away land.

Shoghi Effendi[8]

Exercises

Over the next two weeks, memorize the following:

> The most effective way for them to carry on their work is for the individual to make many contacts, select a few whom they feel would become Bahá'ís, develop a close friendship with them, then complete confidence, and finally teach them the Faith, until they become strong supporters of the Cause of God.
>
> *Shoghi Effendi*[9]

1. How will you *make many contacts*? (What is a contact?)

2. What criteria will you use to *select a few whom they feel would become Bahá'ís*? (This is not an assessment or judgement of one's potential spirituality, it is an assessment of your relationship.)

3. In what ways will you *develop a close friendship with them*?

4. What does *complete confidence* look like with another person?

5. How will you determine the method to *finally teach them the Faith*?

6. How will you know that they have become *strong supporters of the Cause of God*?

5

The Success of the Spiritual Enterprise

Conditions for success: What is the 'one thing'?

Not by the force of numbers, not by the mere exposition of a set of new and noble principles, not by an organized campaign of teaching – no matter how worldwide and elaborate in its character – not even by the staunchness of our faith or the exaltation of our enthusiasm, can we ultimately hope to vindicate in the eyes of a critical and sceptical age the supreme claim of the Abhá Revelation. One thing and only one thing will unfailingly and alone secure the undoubted triumph of this sacred Cause, namely, the extent to which our own inner life and private character mirror forth in their manifold aspects the splendor of those eternal principles proclaimed by Baháʾuʾlláh.

Shoghi Effendi[1]

Splendour: Magnificent in appearance, grandeur; magnificent features and qualities. Its origin is from the Latin, *splendere*, 'to shine, be bright'. The *one thing* requires us to manifest in our private character the splendour of the principles that have been proclaimed by Baháʾuʾlláh and that we have dedicated our lives to obtain and live by. In other words, those around us must see these principles shining out brightly from us in our daily interactions. Without this splendour, our activities will bear no fruit.

Einstein wrote about the tendency we have, to feel 'separate from the rest' of humanity: 'A human being is a part of the whole, called by us "Universe," a part limited in time and space. He experiences himself, his thoughts and feelings as something separate from the rest – a kind of optical delusion of his consciousness.'[2]

The light, or lack thereof, is reflected in our interactions with others. The more the splendour of the teachings of our Faith shines brightly within us and outwardly to others, the more those qualities will be reflected in receptive souls. For the soul, like the moth, seeks the light. These interactions confirm to us that we are 'as one soul in many bodies'.

This reflection in others is something that we can learn to recognize and then proceed with meaningful conversations and interactions. It is through this interaction that we can find avenues to connect with the hearts of those with whom we come into contact. It is the power of this connection that sometimes causes us to pause and step back rather than recognize it and go forward. It is a connection that exists throughout the physical world as well, as Fritjof Capra pointed out:

> Quantum physics thus reveals a basic oneness of the universe. It shows that we cannot decompose the world into independently existing smallest units. As we penetrate into matter, nature does not show us any isolated 'building blocks', but rather appears as a complicated web of relations between the various parts of the whole.[3]

The recognition of our essential oneness and meditation on this pivotal principle enables us to gain the confirmation and confidence to seek out new people, engage in meaningful and uplifting conversations – to go where we may have never gone before.

In the early 1990s, I was asked by the National Spiritual Assembly of the Bahá'ís of the United States to join a short-term task force on race in America. We were charged to address a few issues on race and race relations. I felt inadequate to participate, but that had never stopped me before, so I jumped in.

The group included people from various ethnic, racial and age groups. As with most groups, our initial meeting began with the sharing of backgrounds, exploring where one another's passions were and speaking about our individual experiences. We began in earnest to delve into the questions asked of us to explore by the National Spiritual Assembly in the afternoon of the first day. Most of us had never met each other before this gathering.

The afternoon discussion was slow, and for me a bit boring. As one who seldom hesitates to stir the pot and explore the uncomfortable, I expressed a position on an issue that did not sit so well with others. I have always felt that although I may often be wrong, I am seldom in doubt. Not intentionally to ever be offensive, this time I had come very close to the line for some of the participants. We took a short break for coffee and refreshments.

On the break, Jenise Gaertner approached me. 'We need to talk,' she said in a rather stern voice. Jenise was a large, rather overweight black woman from east Los Angeles with a commanding and intimidating presence. 'Even though you are a bit naive on that issue, I like your passion on the subject.'

Although I feigned offence at her attack, I said, 'Ok, tell me more!' Thus began a great friendship and deep love for one another. I had found a fountain of knowledge and experience that influences me to this day.

Jenise and I spent the rest of the afternoon in the back of the room conversing. The meeting seemed to drag on and we were deep in private conversation. Jenise mentioned a concept that although I was familiar with the behaviour and completely recognized it, I had never heard the term *white privilege* before. She spoke with passion and clarity, without prejudice and in a stern, but loving tone.

She commented to me that she noticed that I had no lack of hesitation to engage in this rather intense conversation, and my complete ease and comfort about speaking on the topic of race. I explained to her that I had, in this new terminology, a very different kind of white privilege that no one of my peers growing up had experienced. She asked, with a bit of scepticism, what that was,

I told her that I had grown up in both the white and black communities since I was a toddler. I loved and was loved by both the white, Jewish community in which I lived and the black community where my father's business was. I came from Cleveland, Ohio. In the 1950s, Cleveland was a very large industrial city and almost completely segregated by ethnicity or race. My father was the only white business owner in what was considered the 'roughest' and most dangerous section of Cleveland. His business was the only business in the area that never had a robbery. When I was a young teenager, I was told by someone in the black neighbourhood the reason. He said, 'Your father's business is off limits.' I asked why. 'He takes care of the people in this neighbourhood. He is family and if anyone needs something, Maury lends a hand, lends money, gives a hearing ear.'

When I went to my father's business to hang out from time to time, since the time I was a young boy, people in the neighbourhood would grab my hand and take me for a walk and give a shout to my dad, 'Hey, Maury, I'll bring him back some time.' People would shout out to whoever was walking me, 'Hey, is that Maury's boy?' My father never worried about me and would let me go off with some person he didn't really know very well, but recognized from the neighbourhood, and knew I would be fine.

I knew no person my age, in my neighbourhood, who had had that experience. That was my real white privilege.

It was quite difficult for me to have an open discussion with anyone I knew who was white. First of all, many white people find the discussion extremely uncomfortable. Second, I have never considered myself as white, and struggled myself with racial prejudice as a Jew. I found having a deep discussion on race with people of colour fairly easy, although sometimes it was not often a well-received opportunity initially.

Jenise had an intimate way of opening a difficult discussion on race without putting the non-minority in a position of guilt or defensiveness. She had a tough, uncompromising manner that was strangely inviting. I learned from her how to engage people who were normally defensive on issues of race in an inviting manner that would encourage hope and uncover the possibility of being successful at it. I finally learned how to engage white people in race discussions without causing distance or offence. That was Jenise's gift to me. She was able to engage with a 'pure, kindly and radiant heart'.

Jenise and I met over the several months the task force consulted. I grew to admire her more and more and learned so much from that joyous and deeply insightful friendship. Unfortunately she passed away young in life from her many health difficulties that plagued her throughout her life. Jenise was a warrior in the army of race harmony, a fearless advocate for racial justice and dedicated to the guidance from the Bahá'í Faith and its institutions.

Another story, which I myself heard from one the Bahá'ís, is this:

We were in a training session as Assistants for Auxiliary Board Member Mrs Javidukht Khadem, the wife of the Hand of the Cause of God, Mr Zikrullah Khadem. She mentioned that 'it is important as an Assistant and as a person, to love others. But it is far more important to let others love you. To love others, we first look within ourselves and find out what we need to be loving. To let others love us, the focus is on the other person and our striving to find that which will allow us to manifest what the other person needs in order to love us.'

This is a great gift: to be sensitive to and begin to recognize what another person needs – and then to strive to manifest those qualities that will attract that person to us. It is what leads to meaningful interactions and the beginning of friendship. Unconditional love may be something quite elusive for most of us. But we can begin to strive for selfless love that is focused on the needs of others. The necessity of striving is true in any kind of enterprise – for instance, as modern business 'gurus' point out:

> Based on *studies in elite performance*, it's 'an extraordinarily consistent answer in an incredible number of fields . . . you need to have practiced, to have apprenticed, for 10,000 hours before you get good' [Malcolm Gladwell]. People aren't born geniuses, they get there through effort.
>
> Then there's the larger matter of how you practice . . . author Cal Newport says that what makes ridiculously successful people so successful is they're experts at practicing – they can push themselves to the exact limit of their skillset and thus expand their abilities day after day. If you're not expanding yourself in such a fashion – called *deliberate practice* . . . you'll never be ridiculously successful.[4]

In the same manner, good teachers are not born that way, nor are they necessarily gifted, but they practise and engage until they become successful, and continue to practise and engage to expand their capacity and capabilities. The successful teachers continually teach, strive for understanding and significance, and reflect, reflect, reflect! And then they take more action, reflect and refine!

The successful teacher is also a constant student. He or she seeks out others engaged in the teaching work and struggles to learn as much as possible from other successful teachers. They will attempt new methods, reflect on those attempts, analyse the efficacy or limitations and refine and employ actions that will improve the teaching process. Like the ever-curious research scientist, successful teachers experiment in the laboratory of life and reflect, analyse and refine continuously.

As students of teaching, our learning process must continuously assess the manner in which the eternal principles of our Faith shine through to others in our daily lives. How can we improve the manner in which the splendour of our inner lives and private character mirror forth so as to attract others? Are we allowing ourselves to be vulnerable to others so as to allow them to find ways to love us? As we immerse ourselves more fully in the Writings and guidance of the Faith, as we manifest in ourselves a desire to learn, as we reflect honestly on our progress or lack thereof in the teaching field, we grow in our confidence, we strive more ardently to acquire virtues, and we rely more fully upon the assistance assured for us from on high. The Universal House of Justice writes:

> The friends in every continent are engaged in study of the Writings for the explicit purpose of learning to apply the teachings to the growth of the Faith. Remarkable numbers are now shouldering responsibility for the spiritual vitality of their communities; energetically, they are carrying out those acts of service befitting a healthy pattern of growth. As they have persevered in the field of service to the Cause, maintaining a humble posture of learning, their courage and wisdom, zeal and acuity, fervour and circumspection, determination and trust in God have combined all the more to reinforce one another. In their presentation of the message of Bahá'u'lláh and the exposition of its verities, they have taken to heart the words of Shoghi Effendi that they must neither 'hesitate' nor 'falter', neither 'overstress' nor 'whittle down' the truth which they champion. Neither are they 'fanatical' nor 'excessively liberal'. Through their constancy in teaching, they have increased their ability to determine whether the receptivity of their listener requires them to be 'wary' or 'bold', to 'act swiftly' or to 'mark time', to be 'direct' or 'indirect' in the methods they employ.[5]

Further considerations

Let him not be content until he has infused into his spiritual child so deep a longing as to impel him to arise independently, in his turn, and devote his energies to the quickening of other souls, and the upholding of the laws and principles laid down by his newly adopted Faith.

Shoghi Effendi[6]

Nor should any of the pioneers, at this early stage in the upbuilding of Bahá'í national communities, overlook the fundamental prerequisite for any successful teaching enterprise, which is to adapt the presentation of the fundamental principles of their Faith to the cultural and religious backgrounds, the ideologies, and the temperament of the divers races and nations whom they are called upon to enlighten and attract.

Shoghi Effendi[7]

Exercises

Over the next two weeks, memorize this Hidden Word:

> O Son of Spirit! My first counsel is this: Possess a pure, kindly and radiant heart, that thine may be a sovereignty ancient, imperishable and everlasting.
>
> *Bahá'u'lláh*[8]

1. What are the visible signs of a *pure, kindly and radiant heart*?

2. What evidence would someone see if the splendour of these words became part of your life?

3. What meanings do you derive from the statement of a *sovereignty*?

4. If you could choose three of the eternal principles proclaimed by Bahá'u'lláh that people would see in you, what would they be?

5. How can you acquire them, nurture them and make them a visible splendour to others?

6

One Creation, Two Worlds

Laws of reality and life:

Nourishment and growth

Intone, O My servant, the verses of God that have been received by thee, as intoned by them who have drawn nigh unto Him, that the sweetness of thy melody may kindle thine own soul, and attract the hearts of all men. Whoso reciteth, in the privacy of his chamber, the verses revealed by God, the scattering angels of the Almighty shall scatter abroad the fragrance of the words uttered by his mouth, and shall cause the heart of every righteous man to throb. Though he may, at first, remain unaware of its effect, yet the virtue of the grace vouchsafed unto him must needs sooner or later exercise its influence upon his soul. Thus have the mysteries of the Revelation of God been decreed by virtue of the Will of Him Who is the Source of power and wisdom.

Bahá'u'lláh[1]

Once we have recognized the Manifestation of God for this Day, we begin a serious and lifelong study of the significance of the Revelation for today. We engage in a process of light-sharing with the rest of the world to slowly awaken humankind to the transition that is taking place and invite others to participate in the development of a new world out of the decaying current world. In order to attract others to this monumental and sacrificial work, we must develop within ourselves attributes that mirror forth and shed a brightness to others. These actions require a new discipline and pattern of life so as to both transform ourselves and attract others to join us in our quest. Bahá'u'lláh tells us:

> Be generous in prosperity, and thankful in adversity. Be worthy of the trust of thy neighbor, and look upon him with a bright and friendly face. Be a treasure to the poor, an admonisher to the rich, an answerer of the cry of the needy, a preserver of the sanctity of thy pledge. Be fair in thy judgment, and guarded in thy speech. Be unjust to no man, and show all meekness to all men. Be as a lamp unto them that walk in darkness, a joy to the sorrowful, a sea for the thirsty, a haven for the distressed, an upholder and defender of the victim of oppression. Let integrity and uprightness distinguish all thine acts . . .[2]

Spiritual life and material life require nourishment and growth. The laws of creation demand light, air, water and exercise to nurture both the material and the spiritual. The material laws are well known for the most part. But the application of these same laws to the spirit require investigation and new discipline.

This new discipline requires the same four essential elements in the process of transformation – the same for a spiritual transformation as well as a physical one. They consist of (metaphorically speaking) light, air, water and exercise. The acquisition of each requires a different practice for the spirit from those for the physical body, but are essential for each.

If we again return to the development of the butterfly, we observe the struggle in the transition from caterpillar. This struggle requires these same four essentials in order for the butterfly to begin its flight into its new existence.

When the butterfly is ready to hatch, the chrysalis becomes transparent. The need for restriction has been outgrown. Yet the struggle toward freedom has an organic timing. It is connected to the breath. A children's book states that the butterfly 'pops' its chrysalis by taking a deep, full breath. As the butterfly emerges, it is upside down. It immediately turns right side up and it proceeds to hold its chrysalis with such reverence, one can almost 'hear' it saying 'thank you' to where it came from.

Light brings nutrition and vitamins to the chrysalis, air is needed for the breath of new life, water nurtures the health of the process, and exercise in the struggle to free the butterfly from the cocoon enables flight.

When we've been through troubles or trauma, it can be difficult to find the gratitude for where we came from. It may be empowering to pause and give thanks in our own lives for our multiple transitions on our spiritual journey and recognize the essential practices that we must continue to develop on our never-ending travels.

Once we begin this spiritual path, our lives change in ways we could never imagine. 'Abdu'l-Bahá was said to *walk the spiritual path with practical feet.* Muhammad similarly said to *trust in God, but tie your camel.* Our spiritual path couples with our physical path and one enables the other. And then the fun begins in ways that we can never imagine. For instance:

Just before Mrs. C left the household of 'Abdu'l-Bahá in 'Akka, 'He came into her room to say farewell, and seating Himself by the window looked off upon the sea in silence for so long a time that His guest began to wonder if He had forgotten her presence.

'Then at length He turned to her and said, with that eager speech that is one of His peculiarities: "Mrs. C when you go back to New York talk to people about the love of God. People in the world do not talk enough about God. Their conversation is filled with trivialities, and they forget the most momentous subjects. Yet if you speak to them of God they are happy, and presently they open their hearts to you.

Often you cannot mention this glorious Revelation, for their prejudice would interfere, and they would not listen. But you will find that you can always talk to them about the love of God."

'Then He went away, and Mrs. C sat a long time in the gathering darkness, while the glory of the sun descended upon the glittering waters of the Mediterranean. The fragrant shadows seemed to echo softly with the last words of 'Abdu'l-Bahá: "You will find that you can always talk to them about the love of God."'³

When I was on pilgrimage in 1976, a group of us were sitting in the Pilgrim House near the Shrine of the Báb. There was a pioneer from Africa visiting from a German background. He was asked why he went to pioneer to Africa and said, 'During World War II, I was in the army in Africa under Rommel. When the war ended I returned to Germany and found the Bahá'í Faith. During the Ten Year Plan, I decided to return to Africa as a pioneer and have been there since. During the war, I was one of Rommel's communications officers, so I was fortunate not to have been in any direct combat situations.'

At this, a British Bahá'í who was also present let out a quick laugh. Some of the friends in the room looked at him strangely. He said, 'Excuse me, I didn't mean to laugh, but there is something so funny to me about your story! You see, during the war I, too, was in Africa serving under General Montgomery in the British Army. I was a Bahá'í, and served in a non-combat role. After the war, also during the Ten Year Plan, I decided to pioneer back to Africa as well.' And, after a short pause, he said, 'I was one of Montgomery's communications officers.'

The two men had never met as they were in different countries pioneering and only met then in the Pilgrimage House in Haifa next to the Shrine of the Báb! Neither of them could have imagined how their lives would be transformed as they travelled through the changes and chances thrust upon them. As they developed the discipline of the spirit and sought out a life of service, each found the fulfilment their hearts desired. They met at the Holy Shrines as true brothers. Bahá'u'lláh writes:

> Regard man as a mine rich in gems of inestimable value. Education can, alone, cause it to reveal its treasures, and enable mankind to benefit therefrom.[4]

Further considerations

The birds of men's hearts, however high they soar, can never hope to attain the heights of His unknowable Essence. It is He Who hath called into being the whole of creation, Who hath caused every created thing to spring forth at His behest.

Bahá'u'lláh[5]

The fundamental principle enunciated by Bahá'u'lláh . . . is that religious truth is not absolute but relative, that Divine Revelation is a continuous and progressive process, that all the great religions of the world are divine in origin, that their basic principles are in complete harmony, that their aims and purposes are one and the same, that their teachings are but facets of one truth, that their functions are complementary, that they differ only in the nonessential aspects of their doctrines, and that their missions represent successive stages in the spiritual evolution of human society

Shoghi Effendi[6]

Exercises

1. In what ways has your life changed since you began your spiritual journey?

2. What activities do you do now that you did not do before?

3. Which of these activities surprise you and why?

4. What five things (actions, travels, accomplishments, capabilities) would you like to do or acquire in the next five years? What actions will you begin to take to make that happen?

5. Over the next two weeks, memorize the following words of Bahá'u'lláh:

O My servants! Sorrow not if, in these days and on this earthly plane, things contrary to your wishes have been ordained and manifested by God, for days of blissful joy, of heavenly delight, are assuredly in store for you. Worlds, holy and spiritually glorious, will be unveiled to your eyes. You are destined by Him, in this world and hereafter, to partake of their benefits, to share in their joys, and to obtain a portion of their sustaining grace. To each and every one of them you will, no doubt, attain.[7]

7

Into the Light

Belief, recognition, intellectual curiosity

But education is of three kinds: material, human, and spiritual. Material education aims at the growth and development of the body, and consists in securing its sustenance and obtaining the means of its ease and comfort. This education is common to both man and animal.

Human education, however, consists in civilization and progress, that is, sound governance, social order, human welfare, commerce and industry, arts and sciences, momentous discoveries, and great undertakings, which are the central features distinguishing man from the animal.

As to divine education, it is the education of the Kingdom and consists in acquiring divine perfections. This is indeed true education, for by its virtue man becomes the focal centre of divine blessings and the embodiment of the verse 'Let Us make man in Our image, after Our likeness.' This is the ultimate goal of the world of humanity.

'Abdu'l-Bahá[1]

The Chinese Bamboo Tree requires considerable effort. It needs nurturing through water, fertile soil, and much sunshine. After one plants the seed, waters the ground and adds fertilizer, nothing happens for a whole year. There are no visible signs of growth in spite of providing all of these things.

After the second year of watering, fertilizing, and tender care of the soil, again there is no visible growth above the ground. Three years – nothing, four years, again nothing. Nothing visible seems to be occurring. Nothing to show for all the effort!

Great patience is needed and steadfastness is tested. One begins to wonder if all the effort of caring for and watering the tree will ever be rewarded. Doubt sets in and one questions the value of all the effort. Inevitably, many people will start to quit.

But, finally in the fifth year – something amazing happens! The Chinese Bamboo Tree grows 25 metres tall in just six weeks! Some species will grow 100 centimetres or 39 inches per day.

In fact, for the first four years, the little tree grows underground, developing a root system strong enough to support its potential for outward growth in the fifth year and beyond. Had the tree not developed a strong unseen foundation, it could never sustain its future tall structure and withstand the winds and storms that would inevitably come.

A rich variety of moral and spiritual lessons lie hidden in the growth of the Chinese Bamboo. For the individual, the lesson is that we too must build a strong foundation of knowledge, accompanied by volition and action. We must gather knowledge in the arts and sciences, seek divine knowledge through the study of the Holy Texts, and acquire a root system of strength within ourselves to withstand the tests and trials that life thrusts upon us.

Shoghi Effendi states that the building of the Faith appears to be 'slow and unobtrusive':

> It is this building process, slow and unobtrusive, to which the life of the world-wide Bahá'í Community is wholly consecrated, that constitutes the one hope of a stricken society. For this process is actuated by the generating influence of God's changeless Purpose, and is evolving within the framework of the Administrative Order of His Faith.[2]

Like the growth of the Chinese Bamboo, the Faith must grow and nurture its foundation. It began with the development of small clusters of individuals. This advanced into the development of small communities and the initiation of its administrative institutions. As these clusters and communities grew, there began a process of collective action invested in the core activities of the institute process: the devotional gatherings, study circles, children's classes and junior youth empowerment programme. This process expands the growth to the outward community and begins to express the Teachings into a forest of community action and service. This, in turn, advances the external growth of the Spirit of the Age in the world.

As in all areas of life, growth depends on light. Light begins with heat, which perpetuates the flowing of photons (in Einstein's vernacular) and thus, emanation. It brings life to existence in the material world. In the mental and spiritual worlds, light, from the heat of love (attraction), knowledge and understanding enriches the growth of the individual and society.

One of the main disciplines of the growth of the spirit is the constant intellectual curiosity to investigate reality. We must strive to advance within ourselves all three kinds of education: material, human, and spiritual.

> Arts, crafts and sciences uplift the world of being, and are conducive to its exaltation. Knowledge is as wings to man's life, and a ladder for his ascent. Its acquisition is incumbent upon everyone. The knowledge of such sciences, however, should be acquired as can profit the peoples of the earth, and not those which begin with words and end with words.[3]

The idea of not expending time and energy on things which begin with words and end with words can be applied in much of our lives as well in the pursuit of arts, crafts and sciences.

Our energies must be expended on that which is of benefit to the world, not just to our physical desires or mental exercises. Even in recreation, we should have as a goal to refresh ourselves, uplift our spirits and build our strength so we can continue to serve the betterment of the world.

Through our pursuit of knowledge, we not only feed our intellect, but we open our spirit to what Carl Jung, the famed psychiatrist, calls *synchronicity* – those events that are 'meaningful coincidences' if they occur with no causal relationship yet seem to be meaningfully related. This concept is also mentioned in the Bahá'í Writings, which stress that after prayer, for example, we meditate and then act on that which comes to our minds that seems like an answer to our prayers. The synchronicity between our praying and the inspiration or intuition that follows helps us in our decision-making that is often not a direct response to empirical data.

Alexander Fleming was an inventor and research scientist. In 1928, while working in his home laboratory he and his wife decided to go on vacation. In an oversight, Fleming left a half-completed experiment on bacteria in a petri dish in the lab sink. Upon his return he found that the bacteria had grown all over the plate, except in an area where mould had formed. This accident led to the discovery of penicillin.

I once asked an inventor, What is the biggest factor in your success?' He said, 'By far, even more than persistence and intuition, is to expect serendipity! One must be persistent and try many different things. One must also not ignore intuition, as that is your subconscious playing with patterns that you consciously don't perceive. And we must look at failures as learning exercises. But expecting serendipity, the unexpected or unintended result, makes the invention come to life in unpredictable and delightful ways. It brings joy and wonder to invention.'

The other mode of the spirit's influence and action is without these bodily instruments and organs. For example, in the state of sleep, it sees without eyes, it hears without ears, it speaks without a tongue, it runs without feet – in brief, all these powers are exerted without the mediation of instruments and organs. How often it happens that the spirit has a dream in the realm of sleep whose purport comes to be exactly materialized two years hence! Likewise, how often it happens that in the world of dreams the spirit solves a problem that it could not solve in the realm of wakefulness. Awake, the eye sees only a short distance, but in the realm of dreams one who is in the East may see the West. Awake, he sees only the present; in sleep he beholds the future. Awake, by the fastest means he travels at most seventy miles in an hour; in sleep he traverses East and West in the blink of an eye. For the spirit has two modes of travel: without means, or spiritual travel, and with means, or material travel – as birds that fly, or as being carried in a vehicle.[4]

Albert Einstein is reported as saying: 'The important thing is to not stop questioning. Curiosity has its own reason for existing.'

There was a young man on a journey to Morocco from Ohio in the United States to engage in an illegal business venture. While travelling through Spain on his way, he heard a voice in the middle of a crowd of people that said, 'Return to California, great danger awaits you in Morocco.' He turned to his friend who was travelling with him and said, 'Did you hear that voice?' 'What voice?' his friend responded.

The voice shook him deeply. He abandoned his illegal pursuit and returned to America. On his way to California, he stopped in Ohio to gather his belongings and prepare for his journey. While still in Ohio, his cousin invited him to a retreat to study with the followers of a guru from India. He was not interested in spiritual pursuits, but the experience of the voice prompted him to go. While at the retreat, he recognized the insincerity of the guru's teachings and did not participate. However, while alone he picked up a book enti-tled *The Bhagavad Gita*. In the two days at the retreat, he read the complete book. Upon finishing it, he thought to himself, 'Although these teachings are different from those that I studied as a child in synagogue, the Message is the same.'

After the weekend retreat, he met another friend who had recently returned from Israel where she had been baptized in the Sea of Galilee and converted to Christianity from Judaism. She quite radiantly encouraged the young man to read the New Testament. So he did.

After completing the reading of the New Testament, he accepted Christ. But he also determined from the language in the Revelation of St John, that either Christ had returned and we had missed Him again, or He was walking on the earth presently, or He was coming very soon.

Again, the voice he had heard in Madrid spoke to him and said, 'Go to California!' So he gathered his belongings and set out to California to respond to the voice and to find the return of Christ. He studied the New Testament daily and read it cover to cover several times over the course of the next couple of weeks on his journey across the country.

He had many encounters on his way to California as he hitch-hiked across the vast land. In Wisconsin, he met two young men who housed him overnight and bought him break-fast one morning. They asked him about his life and what he was doing. He told them of his quest to find the return of Christ. The two young men were Bahá'ís and invited him to hear the latest album of a famous band, Seals and Crofts. They listened to the young man tell his story and when it was time to leave, they wished him well and said, 'We hope you find what you are looking for.' They did not tell him of their Faith as they recognized that the young man's cup was overflowing with his newly found recognition of Christ.

On his way out of Wisconsin he got a ride from another group of young people travelling around the country. During the ride, the young man told the group that he was seeking the return of Christ. One of the young women in the group said to him, 'I have a book that I think you would like.' He responded,'"I have the only book I need,' and showed her his Bible. When they finally left him at the highway to continue his journey, the young woman asked him to please take the book as a gift from her. So, not to be rude, he took it and placed it deep underneath his things in his backpack.

On another ride through Texas, being bored with the long ride, tired of reading the Bible, he reached into his backpack and pulled out the book that the young woman gave him. 'I guess a mystery novel will pass the time.' He said to himself. The book was called, *Thief in the Night: The Case of the Missing Millennium*, by William Sears.

He read the book cover to cover in about two hours and was speechless for another several. Instead of a normal mystery novel, this was the story of the return of Christ! He had found what he was looking for.

After another day, he was in California at his parents' home. However, after long meditation, he was again uncertain of the Return. Who is this man, William Sears? Anyone can put together a story and manipulate dates and facts. He had spent too much time 'in the streets' to just accept someone's opinion.

So the young man went to find more information. He finally collected five books on the Bahá'í Faith from a bookstore and the library: *The Wine of Astonishment* and *Release the Sun* by this same William Sears; *Gleanings from the Writings of Bahá'u'lláh, The Proclamation of Bahá'u'lláh,* and *Some Answered Questions* by 'Abdu'l-Bahá. He spent three days in his room at his parents' home and when finished, said, 'Ok, Bahá'u'lláh, I accept. Now what do I do? Are there special clothes to be worn, do I shave my beard or what?'

So, for a month he looked everywhere for Bahá'ís and could not find any. Finally, since he had no money, he decided to sell his motorcycle. He put an ad in the paper and only one person responded. He wanted a bit more than the buyer was prepared to pay. 'My family and I just returned from Argentina and this is all that I can afford. Take it or not,' said the man. So, he thought, it was a fair offer and took it.

When they went to the Department of Motor Vehicles to transfer the papers, the buyer went inside to change the papers while the young man waited outside Sitting on his black Harley Davidson, wearing his black Harley Davidson leather jacket and Castro hat, with full-length beard and shoulder-length hair, he looked at the wife of the man purchasing the motorcycle, and asked, 'Your husband said you just returned from Argentina. Why were you there?' She looked at him with a bit of fear and suspicion and said, 'We were pioneers for the Bahá'í Faith.'

He couldn't believe what he heard. 'I am a Bahá'í!! I know all about Quddús and Mullá Ḥusayn and the struggles at Fort Ṭabarsí! I have been searching for the Bahá'ís!'

The woman was amazed and speechless. After gaining her voice, she invited him to a meeting that evening at the home of one of the local believers. When the young man reached the meeting, he was introduced to the speaker for the evening, Mr William Sears. Mr Sears had just returned from Iran and was showing photographs of all of the historic places in Iran that he had written about in *Release the Sun*.

Of course, that was the beginning of a new life for the young man. The light of his search burned brightly indeed! As Bahá'u'lláh has written:

> So powerful is the light of unity that it can illuminate the whole earth.[5]

Further considerations

Of all the arts and sciences, set the children to studying those which will result in advantage to man, will ensure his progress and elevate his rank. Thus the noisome odours of lawlessness will be dispelled, and thus through the high endeavours of the nation's leaders, all will live cradled, secure and in peace.

Bahá'u'lláh[6]

The sciences of today are bridges to reality; if then they lead not to reality, naught remains but fruitless illusion.

'Abdu'l-Bahá[7]

O Son of Man! The light hath shone on thee from the horizon of the sacred Mount and the spirit of enlightenment hath breathed in the Sinai of thy heart. Wherefore, free thyself from the veils of idle fancies and enter into My court, that thou mayest be fit for everlasting life and worthy to meet Me. Thus may death not come upon thee, neither weariness nor trouble.

Bahá'u'lláh[8]

O Son of Spirit! With the joyful tidings of light I hail thee: rejoice! To the court of holiness I summon thee; abide therein that thou mayest live in peace for evermore.

Bahá'u'lláh[9]

One word may be likened unto fire, another unto light, and the influence which both exert is manifest in the world. Therefore an enlightened man of wisdom should primarily speak with words as mild as milk, that the children of men may be nurtured and edified thereby and may attain the ultimate goal of human existence which is the station of true understanding and nobility. And likewise He saith: One word is like unto springtime causing the tender saplings of the rose-garden of knowledge to become verdant and flourishing, while another word is even as a deadly poison. It behoveth a prudent man of wisdom to speak with utmost leniency and forbearance so that the sweetness of his words may induce everyone to attain that which befitteth man's station.

Bahá'u'lláh[10]

Exercises

Over the next two weeks, memorize the following:

> Arts, crafts and sciences uplift the world of being, and are
> conducive to its exaltation. Knowledge is as wings to man's
> life, and a ladder for his ascent.
>
> *Bahá'u'lláh*[11]

1. Choose an area of arts, crafts or sciences that you are interested in. What would you like to learn about in that area over the course of the next month? How will you learn? (Take a course, seek an expert? Find a course on the Internet?)

2. In what ways will you apply this new learning to your teaching activities?

3. Search for a quotation in the Writings that applies to this new learning.

4. Share your chosen area of learning, and its relationship to the quotation you found, with a friend and engage in a meaningful conversation about your newly gained knowledge.

8

Breath of Life

Prayer and radiant acquiescence

Regard man as a mine rich in gems of inestimable value. Education can, alone, cause it to reveal its treasures, and enable mankind to benefit therefrom. Bahá'u'lláh[1]

In our travels so far in this book, we have identified the four big questions that we must investigate, answer and pursue throughout our lives. We must strive for individual investigation of truth through arts, crafts and sciences and the study of the Holy Texts, accompanied by actions for the betterment of society that enable our spirits to grow and mature.

The lifelong investigation of these questions is furthered by our actions, reflections and refinement in the pursuit of the betterment of the world. We need the light of the sun for our physical growth and the light of the intellect for our spiritual growth. Now we will investigate the air and breath necessary for the enabling of the lifeblood of our souls to flourish.

When drawing the distinction between the animal and the human one realizes that in material areas, the animal is mostly superior. However, the animal cannot change its circumstance. If it is water-bound, it cannot survive outside of the water. If it is land-bound, it cannot fly. However, the human can arise above its material limitations and develop capacities that enable him or her to fly, survive under water, breathe where there is no oxygen.

All of these signs of the human capacity arise from man's greatest capacity – which is self-awareness and the ability to recognize its Creator.

After the recognition of the Creator and His Manifestation for the Day, one begins to walk a spiritual path with practical feet. The one possessed with faith desires to serve humanity, grow capacity to enrich and enlarge the capabilities for service, and to strive to obtain greater understanding of the significance of the Teachings of the Sun of Reality. 'Abdu'l-Bahá writes:

> The Graces of the Kingdom of Abhá are the rays of the Sun of Reality. It illumines the earth and heaven, makes the star a shining moon, turns the speck into a huge mountain, bestows strength to the weak, gives everlasting healing to the sick, grants heavenly treasures to the poor, confirms the oppressed ones to everlasting glory and turns the people of darkness to those of light. [2]

A key enabler for spiritual growth requires learning about prayer, learning how to pray, and putting prayer into daily practice as the food necessary for the soul.

Hand of the Cause of God Abu'l-Qásim Faizi is reported as saying in a talk given in Melbourne, Australia:

> To me, many of the hard problems of all the religions of God have been explained by the Báb, very easily. He brought these things from heaven to earth, and said this is what it means . . .
>
> Why do we pray? The Báb says: When we pray, what do we take to God? What do we talk to Him of, what do we offer Him? Do you offer your knowledge? He is the Source of knowledge. Do you offer Him your wealth? Do you offer Him your strength, the strength of body or mental strength? All these things are not even worthy of being mentioned in the sight of God.

Therefore, why do we pray? The Báb says, I will give you an example. Suppose you want to go and visit a king. You will go here and there and ask many people: what is it that the king does not have in his treasury? I would like to take it as a gift to him. And, for instance, suppose somebody will say if you take a moonstone, he does not have it, then you will take it.

Now, if you take the whole treasure of the world, God has it. The whole knowledge of the world – He is the source of it. Strength? He is the source of power. But the Báb says: I advise you and tell you, there is one thing that God does not have in His treasure house, and that is NOTHINGNESS. Take your nothingness to Him. When you sit down in front of Him and pray, have an attitude that you are nothing as compared with God. You take that attitude, and He says this will immediately be accepted.[3]

And Shoghi Effendi has written:

For the core of religious faith is that mystic feeling which unites Man with God. This state of spiritual communion can be brought about and maintained by means of meditation and prayer. And this is the reason why Bahá'u'lláh has so much stressed the importance of worship. It is not sufficient for a believer to merely accept and observe the teachings. He should, in addition, cultivate the sense of spirituality which he can acquire chiefly by means of prayer. The Bahá'í Faith, like all other Divine Religions, is thus fundamentally mystic in character. Its chief goal is the development of the individual and society, through the acquisition of spiritual virtues and powers. It is the soul of man that has first to be fed. And this spiritual nourishment prayer can best provide.

Laws and institutions, as viewed by Bahá'u'lláh, can become really effective only when our inner spiritual life has been perfected and transformed. Otherwise religion will degenerate into a mere organization, and become a dead thing.[4]

A well-known story about prayer comes from when 'Abdu'l-Bahá was in America in 1912:

> He called to Him an ardent Bahá'í and said, 'If you will come to Me at dawn tomorrow, I will teach you to pray.'
>
> Delighted, Mr. M arose at four and crossed the city, arriving for his lesson at six. With what exultant expectation he must have greeted this opportunity! He found 'Abdu'l-Bahá already at prayer, kneeling by the side of the bed. Mr. M followed suit, taking care to place himself directly across.
>
> Seeing that 'Abdu'l-Bahá was quite lost in His Own reverie, Mr. M began to pray silently for his friends, his family and finally for the crowned heads of Europe. No word was uttered by the quiet Man before him. He went over all the prayers he knew then, and repeated them twice, three times – still no sound broke the expectant hush.
>
> Mr. M surreptitiously rubbed one knee and wondered vaguely about his back. He began again, hearing as he did so, the birds heralding the dawn outside the window. An hour passed, and finally two. Mr. M was quite numb now. His eyes, roving along the wall, caught sight of a large crack. He dallied with a touch of indignation but let his gaze pass again to the still figure across the bed.
>
> The ecstasy that he saw arrested him and he drank deeply of the sight. Suddenly he wanted to pray like that. Selfish desires were forgotten. Sorrow, conflict, and even his immediate surroundings were as if they had never been. He was conscious of only one thing, a passionate desire to draw near to God.
>
> Closing his eyes again he set the world firmly aside, and amazingly his heart teemed with prayer, eager, joyous, tumultuous prayer. He felt cleansed by humility and lighted by a new peace. 'Abdu'l-Bahá had taught him to pray!
>
> The 'Master of 'Akká' immediately arose and came to him. His eyes rested smilingly upon the newly humbled Mr. M.

'When you pray,' He said, 'you must not think of your aching body, nor of the birds outside the window, nor of the cracks in the wall!'

He became very serious then, and added, 'When you wish to pray you must first know that you are standing in the presence of the Almighty!'[5]

Once we learn and begin the practice of prayer, we begin to acquire a pattern of behaviour that draws upon both the material and the spiritual world. Prayer and meditation bring divine confirmations on one hand and material insight on the other. We tap into the quiet around us and begin to hear with a new ear, see with a new eye, speak with a new tongue and understand with a new wisdom.

As 'Abdu'l-Bahá says, we begin to see the end in the beginning. We recognize that in our tests and difficulties, the process of refinement of the soul brings us increased understanding and compassion. We begin to approach the oneness of mankind that we so easily speak of without the recognition of its depth nor the complexity of its inference. Our lives are transformed and we begin to see all of humanity in need of spiritual awakening and that all souls have the capacity to approach the Divine.

With the discipline of daily prayer, we acquire a spiritual orientation to our lives. We learn to respond to our situations in ways that we could not imagine earlier – with 'radiant acquiescence'. In extreme situations, we draw upon a spiritual reservoir and will act with a dignity that we may not be aware of normally. We become receptive to a spiritual dimension in addition to the material dimension.

Illustrating this, among the many stories of the experiences of the Bahá'ís in Iran is this one:

In 1996, one of the young Bahá'ís of the city of Kerman in Iran had just started his mandatory military service in his town. One day he was approached by one of the mullás (priests) who are resident at military garrisons to provide spiritual guidance to the soldiers.

This mullá was referred to as 'Haji' (one who has made his pilgrimage to Mecca) and when he found out that this young man was a Bahá'í, he approached him and instructed him to publicly announce at next morning's prayer assembly that he was a Bahá'í so that everyone would know.

The young Bahá'í agreed to comply. The next morning when all the soldiers assembled for morning prayers and received the day's instructions the young Bahá'í went in front of the crowd, and with respect and dignity announced that he had been instructed by Haji to tell everyone that he was a Bahá'í in case anyone would wish not to associate with him because of his being a Bahá'í.

When he had returned to his duties, Haji approached him again. With great anger he said, 'I told you to only say that you are a Bahá'í. I didn't ask you to give a lecture and tell them why. Now you must be punished.'

He instructed the other men to throw the young Bahá'í into a lavatory and keep him locked there until further instructions. So they locked up the young Bahá'í and kept him there except for giving him a little food every day. Almost two weeks had passed when one night this young Bahá'í soldier had a dream in which 'Abdu'l-Bahá addressed him in these words: 'You have passed your test very well.'

The next morning soldiers opened the door and in a great hurry took him to meet the Haji. When they entered the room, the Haji seemed very shaken and upset. In a trembling voice, he said: 'The reason I released you from detention is that last night I had a very vivid dream in which a turbaned Siyyid (a descendant of the Prophet Muhammad) addressed me and said: "Why have you imprisoned my son? You only have three days to release him and ask for his forgiveness." So, I am releasing you,' the Haji said, 'and I am begging for your forgiveness. I will not let you go until you have forgiven me.'

The young Bahá'í said that he already had forgiven him.

Exactly three days later, the Haji died. Just before his passing he had told the story of the young Bahá'í soldier to his wife and children and had said to them, 'Follow the way and example of this youth for the rest of your lives.'[6]

Further considerations

It is not desirable that a man be left without knowledge or skills, for he is then but a barren tree. Then, so much as capacity and capability allow, ye needs must deck the tree of being with fruits such as knowledge, wisdom, spiritual perception and eloquent speech. *Bahá'u'lláh*[7]

We should continually be establishing new bases for human happiness and creating and promoting new instrumentalities toward this end. How excellent, how honourable is man if he arises to fulfil his responsibilities; how wretched and contemptible, if he shuts his eyes to the welfare of society and wastes his precious life in pursuing his own selfish interests and personal advantages. Supreme happiness is man's, and he beholds the signs of God in the world and in the human soul, if he urges on the steed of high endeavor in the arena of civilization and justice. *'Abdu'l-Bahá*[8]

O Lord, help Thou Thy loved ones to acquire knowledge and the sciences and arts, and to unravel the secrets that are treasured up in the inmost reality of all created beings. Make them to hear the hidden truths that are written and embedded in the heart of all that is.

'Abdu'l-Bahá[9]

The primary, the most urgent requirement is the promotion of education. It is inconceivable that any nation should achieve prosperity and success unless this paramount, this fundamental concern is carried forward. The principal reason for the decline and fall of peoples is ignorance. Today the mass of the people are uninformed even as to ordinary affairs, how much less do they grasp the core of the important problems and complex needs of the time.

'Abdu'l-Bahá[10]

Exercises

1. In the next two weeks, choose a prayer (one that you have not memorized before) and memorize it.

2. Over the next month, say this newly memorized prayer every day.

3. How has the reciting of this prayer daily affected your thoughts, your actions, your conversations? What insights have you gained in meditation after saying this prayer?

4. What new insights have you gained over the month that surprise you and bring you joy?

5. Engage in a meaningful conversation with a friend about the new insight and understanding. Share in what ways this prayer has brought this insight and understanding to you. If possible and appropriate, share the prayer with your friend.

6. Describe the results of this conversation. In what ways do you think the conversation affected your friend?

9
Water of Life
Memorization for confirmation

The sanctified souls should ponder and meditate in their hearts regarding the methods of teaching. From the texts of the wondrous, heavenly Scriptures they should memorize phrases and passages bearing on various instances, so that in the course of their speech they may recite divine verses whenever the occasion demandeth it, inasmuch as these holy verses are the most potent elixir, the greatest and mightiest talisman. So potent is their influence that the hearer will have no cause for vacillation.

Bahá'u'lláh[1]

The physical sun imparts light to bring life to the planet. The Sun of Reality imparts spiritual light to bring life to the soul. We breathe in the physical air to sustain our lives and breathe in the Word of God to sustain our spiritual life. When we memorize the Word of God, the life-giving waters of the eternal realm permeate our being, affect our daily lives, and bring life to our thoughts, our relationships and our conversations.

As you memorize the Holy Words, your very demeanour changes as the 'sweetness of thy melody may kindle thine own soul, and attract the hearts of all men'.[2] This enkindlement affects our relationships, attracts others to us and enables our confidence.

In our desire to uplift our relationships with others, the words we use can have a profound effect on every conversation we engage in.

In 1954, in response to the call for pioneers during the Ten Year Crusade of the beloved Guardian Shoghi Effendi, Frederick (Fred) and Elizabeth (Beth) Laws arose and moved to Lesotho, in Southern Africa. As they left their home country, they put on the mantle of the Words of Bahá'u'lláh, memorized a few passages to give them confidence in the Holy Spirit's assistance and began their travels.

Travelling through a mountainous region looking for a place to settle, they came upon a lovely home with trees planted in the compound around the house. There were almost no trees, Lesotho having been stripped of its trees during the height of the colonial period. They stopped in front of the house and got out of the car to look around.

Chadwick and Mary Mohapi owned the land and the house. Chadwick, wondering who these European-looking people were and why they were standing in front of his house, sent one of his sons to go and find out. Chadwick was in his 60s and was retired after serving many years in several different jobs throughout his country.

Chadwick had been a mechanic for automobiles, heating and cooling systems and water systems. He had worked as a chauffeur to one of the guards of the royal family at one time, and many other types of work over his lifetime. He had served in the armed forces during World War I and went to Europe where he fell in love with the trees and vowed to plant trees in his beloved Lesotho. Over his lifetime, he planted many trees.

When Chadwick and Mary's son Selai went out to meet this couple standing outside the compound, Fred and Beth introduced themselves to the boy. Chadwick and Mary came out and asked why they were there and what they wanted. Fred and Beth asked if they could use a portion of the stone wall around the compound and put up a canvas. With a bit of suspicion, Chadwick asked why. 'So we can have a place to sleep for a bit until our things arrive and we find a place to settle.'

As a joke, Chadwick invited them to stay in a thatched-roof

hut inside the compound and live there until they found a place. He was sure that a white person would never want to live with an African family. But, to his surprise and consternation, they accepted and said that they would very much appreciate that. So, Chadwick and Mary were stuck and had to invite them in.

The Laws said that they would return with their things shortly and looked forward to staying there. Of course, the Mohapis thought that would be the end of that. But a bit later the Laws returned with their things and moved into the small one-room hut. Fred and Beth invited Chadwick and Mary to come to the hut for dinner that first night. Taken aback, they accepted with not just a little bit of fear.

The next morning, the Laws invited the Mohapis for breakfast. On the third day, the Mohapis realized the sincerity of this 'European' couple (as all whites were called). They asked them, 'Why are you here in Lesotho?'

Chadwick and Mary were descendants of royal families and were honoured citizens of Lesotho. They accepted the Faith in a short time after meeting with the Laws and served with great distinction for the rest of their lives. Both Chadwick and Mary travelled extensively throughout Lesotho and other neighbouring countries. Many people embraced the Faith because of their ceaseless devotion and teaching of the Cause. At Chadwick's passing (a decade after his beloved Mary) over 800 people, from the royal Queen to high-ranking officials to farmers and workers, came to pay homage to the beloved first believer of the Bahá'í Faith in Lesotho.

The Laws were filled with the Words of Bahá'u'lláh. From their hearts they imparted the spirit of the Faith. They infused the Mohapis with the love of the Faith, which they, in turn, taught so many others throughout the southern African countries.

The Mohapis were attracted to Fred and Beth at a time when there was much suspicion and mistrust between the whites and the Africans in Africa. It was dangerous to associate with one another, let alone become friends and live in close proximity. But Shoghi Effendi had directed the pioneers to southern Africa to teach the Africans and the coloured people, but not the whites – to pick the choicest fruit, which in any region is the indigenous fruit. The Laws were obedient and loving and the results reflected their obedience.[3]

'Abdu'l-Bahá's words, expressed many times in the same vein during the First World War, are quoted in a letter to an early American believer:

> Have patience – wait, but do not sit idle; work while you are waiting; smile while you are wearied with monotony; be firm while everything around you is being shaken; be joyous while the ugly face of despair grins at you; speak aloud while the malevolent forces of the nether world try to crush your mind; be valiant and courageous while men all around you are cringing with fear and cowardice. Do not yield to the over-whelming power of tyranny and despotism. Serve the cause of democracy and freedom. Continue your journey to the end. The bright day is coming. The nucleus of the new race is forming. The harbinger of the new ideals of international justice is appearing. The trees of hope will become verdant; the copper of scorn and derision will be transmuted into the gold of honour and praise; the arid desert of ignorance will be transformed into the luxuriant garden of knowledge; the threatening clouds shall be dispelled and the stars of faith and charity will again twinkle in the clear heaven of human consciousness.[4]

When we begin a relationship with someone, it is important that we spend most of our time listening and understanding the other person. Although we know that it is the Holy Words that move the heart, we must use great tact and wisdom not to overwhelm someone before we have developed a relationship with them.

As well, the attraction to another in the process of developing a deep friendship involves a sharing with and disclosure of ourselves. Laughter is a great highway to a heart. I remember always the privilege of spending time with Hands of the Cause of God and what I remember most was each one's sense of humour which often broke through the formality – so that when they became serious, the words penetrated.

There's a story about a little conversation that is supposed to have taken place between two legends, Charles Spencer (Charlie) Chaplin and Albert Einstein, at a public event. It went something like this:

> *Einstein*: What I most admire about your art, is your universality. You don't say a word, yet the world understands you!
>
> *Chaplin*: True. But your glory is even greater! The whole world admires you, even though they don't understand a word of what you say.

Hydrogen and oxygen gases mix at room temperature with no chemical reaction. This is because the speed of the molecules does not provide enough kinetic energy to activate a reaction during collisions between the reactants. However, the introduction of a spark to the mixture results in raised temperatures amongst some of the hydrogen and oxygen molecules. Molecules at higher temperatures travel faster and collide with more energy. If collision energies reach a minimum activation energy sufficient to 'break' the bonds between the reactants, then a reaction between the hydrogen and oxygen follows.

Spiritual bonds are formed in a similar fashion. When two people meet and the heat of that meeting is warmed, a relationship ignites. If the heat generated is accompanied with the heat of a spiritual bonding, it creates an activation of energy that results in a meaningful conversation and connection, and a friendship develops.

William H. (Harry) Randall was a man of wealth and affairs. He had been a classmate of Harlan Ober at Harvard, so when Harlan learned of the Faith and became a Bahá'í, he very soon gave the Message to Harry, only to discover that, busy and occupied as he was with his manifold affairs, Harry's interest went no farther than a polite and courteous response, which was far from satisfactory to Harlan.

He persisted in trying to interest Harry further and when 'Abdu'l-Bahá was to come to Boston, Harlan grew more and more pressing: Harry must go to hear 'Abdu'l-Bahá speak; Harry must meet Him; Harry really owed it to himself not to miss this wonderful opportunity. Finally, Harry still uninterested, but courteously anxious to please this eager friend of his, agreed to go with Harlan to hear 'Abdu'l-Bahá.

Ruth, Harry's wife, would not be able to go with him since she was a semi-invalid, in and out of sanitoriums for tuberculosis a great part of the time. Just then she had come home from one of these hospitals but she was far too frail to do anything but rest quietly at home. Harlan and Harry Randall went to the meeting together and after it was over, Harlan insisted upon taking Harry to meet 'Abdu'l-Bahá. Harry, still uninterested but always courteous, did as Harlan wished.

What was his astonishment when 'Abdu'l-Bahá warmly accepted an invitation to have tea the following afternoon at Harry's home! An invitation Harry had in no way extended. Appalled, Harry asked Harlan what on earth he should do about it? Harlan said. 'Give a tea for Him. What else can you do?' 'But how can I? Ruth is ill. I'm busy. How on earth?'

Harlan laughed, 'You don't know 'Abdu'l-Bahá or you'd know there's some sort of reason for this, and it'll get done. You have a houseful of servants – let them brew a cup of tea for the Master and invite a few friends in to share it.' So this is what Harry did and the next afternoon when 'Abdu'l-Bahá arrived at the lovely suburban home, He found quite a group of people assembled on a wide verandah to receive Him.

Ruth Randall, delicate and lovely, was also there, seated in a far corner where she might be safe from any draft. It was to her, ignoring all the others, that 'Abdu'l-Bahá strode, His white *aba* billowing with the swiftness of His tread; His beautiful eyes filled with light and love. Reaching her He bent above her, murmuring, 'My daughter, My dear daughter,' and lovingly He rested His hands on her shoulders. Then He turned and, smilingly, met all the other guests.

The following day, Ruth had an appointment with her doctor, who had examined her the previous week and had said that it might be necessary for her to return to the sanitorium for further treatment. He would be sure after he had seen her again. Ruth went to this appointment fearfully as she was so longing to remain at home, so very reluctant to be sent again to the hospital. The doctor examined her – and was amazed. What had she been doing? What could have happened to her? She was healed. There was not the least trace left of the tuberculosis.

Of course, this was an experience that neither Harry nor Ruth could ignore, so it was the beginning of their long and glorious lifetime of teaching and serving the Cause they came to love so well. [5]

Harry Randall was later named a Disciple of 'Abdu'l-Bahá, and received a Tablet from Him calling Harry 'my spiritual associate'. [6] He and Ruth were instrumental in the construction of the Western Pilgrim House in Haifa, and later in the development of Green Acre Bahá'í School.

Harlan Ober had persisted in his desire to bring his dear friend, Harry, into the understanding of the Teachings of the Faith. His efforts were rewarded and not only did he have a dear friend, but he now had a spiritual brother. As Shoghi Effendi writes:

Let him not be content until he has infused into his spiritual

child so deep a longing as to impel him to arise independently, in his turn, and devote his energies to the quickening
of other souls, and the upholding of the laws and principles
laid down by his newly adopted Faith.[7]

I like this story of Harry Randall also because it illustrates
another characteristic of 'Abdu'l-Bahá. We normally do not
emphasize that He was an extraordinary Being and could call
upon the Power of God in many ways, not the least of which
was to heal others.

Another story that illustrates the wonder of 'Abdu'l-Bahá
concerns Lua Getsinger, one of the earliest believers in the
West, and an extremely successful teacher of the Faith. Hand
of the Cause of God William Sears once said in a conversation in his home that if all the Bahá'ís in America would
trace their Bahá'í lineage, it would lead back to Lua. There are
many stories about her. Grace Ober, who heard this one from
Lua herself, speaks of a time when Lua was in the Holy Land.
On a walk with 'Abdu'l-Bahá and others on the sands near
'Akká, Lua began to place her feet into the footprints left by
'Abdu'l-Bahá, Who was walking ahead. He asked her several
times, and quite sternly, if she wanted to walk in His foot-
steps, and she replied several times that she did. Suddenly she
was bitten by a large scorpion; her ankle became quite swollen
and very painful. Once back in 'Akká, the Greatest Holy Leaf
attended her, but to no avail, and finally beseeched 'Abdu'l-
Bahá to intervene and heal her. 'Abdu'l-Bahá placed His hands
on Lua's forehead and her temperature slowly drained away.[8]

Lua's life was filled with stories of her desire to live according to the example of 'Abdu'l-Bahá. Not only did she spend
her time learning and memorizing the Holy Text, but she
would earnestly strive to memorize His very actions.

Further considerations

The state of prayer is the best of conditions, for man is then associating with God. Prayer verily bestoweth life, particularly when offered in private and at times, such as midnight, when freed from daily cares.

'Abdu'l-Bahá[9]

These children are even as young plants, and teaching them the prayers is as letting the rain pour down upon them, that they may wax tender and fresh, and the soft breezes of the love of God may blow over them, making them to tremble with joy.

'Abdu'l-Bahá[10]

Make firm our steps, O Lord, in Thy path and strengthen Thou our hearts in Thine obedience. Turn our faces toward the beauty of Thy oneness, and gladden our bosoms with the signs of Thy divine unity. Adorn our bodies with the robe of Thy bounty, and remove from our eyes the veil of sinfulness, and give us the chalice of Thy grace; that the essence of all beings may sing Thy praise before the vision of Thy grandeur. Reveal then Thyself, O Lord, by Thy merciful utterance and the mystery of Thy divine being, that the holy ecstasy of prayer may fill our souls – a prayer that shall rise above words and letters and transcend the murmur of syllables and sounds – that all things may be merged into nothingness before the revelation of Thy splendour.

'Abdu'l-Bahá[11]

Exercises

1. Over the course of the next month, memorize a quotation from the Writings of Bahá'u'lláh, a quotation from 'Abdu'l-Bahá and a quotation from Shoghi Effendi (the quotations can be small or large depending on your choice).

2. Once memorized, say all three quotations daily for two weeks. Over the course of the two weeks, can you begin to distinguish the difference in the voices? What characteristics of each voice can you identify?

3. Begin to read other passages from Bahá'u'lláh, 'Abdu'l-Bahá and Shoghi Effendi. How recognizable are these distinctions that you identified?

4. Over the next months, try to bring these quotations into conversations with your friends, co-workers or fellow believers.

5. How have your conversations changed?

Exercise of the Spiritual Being

Goodly deeds and perseverance

The betterment of the world can be accomplished through pure and goodly deeds, through commendable and seemly conduct.
Bahá'u'lláh[1]

William Tumanvow White was a Samoan believer from Western Samoa. He had the exalted title of Tumanvow which is one of the most honoured titles in his culture. A dedicated believer, he would travel, walking from village to village, to bring the Faith of Bahá'u'lláh to his beloved fellow villagers.

In his youth, Tumanvow had been a strong and well-known boxer. But in his older years he suffered from a tropical disease carried by mosquitos that caused the lower half of his body to swell. Although his life was filled with physical pain, the joy of teaching propelled him to walk around the Western Samoan islands bringing the glad-tidings of Bahá'u'lláh.

Tumanvow and his wife lived a simple life in a small hut with a thatched roof, concrete floor and no walls. All were welcome and he was much loved by friends in all of Western Samoa. He served as an Auxiliary Board member and was asked by the National Spiritual Assembly of Western Samoa to travel to the islands of Samoa and teach. These islands were, in the 1970s, still very tribal. When he arrived, by the occasional boat, to the Tokelau Islands of Samoa, he was told by the authorities that it was best if he did not speak of his religion. Of course, this was the sole purpose for his travelling there.

The authorities, to prevent him from teaching, took him to a deserted end of the island and forbade him to leave until the next boat arrived to take him away. The next boat was in three months. He was assigned a police guard to make sure he stayed there. Religion in the islands was controlled by the Church in conjunction with the civil authorities, and the law allowed the tribal chiefs to control what religions were allowed on the islands.

Tumanvow came from an island rich in a variety of fruits and vegetables. However, on Tokelau only coconuts grew. So, his diet on Tokelau consisted of just coconuts and fish, which caused him great physical stress and raised boils all over his body. His system could not, at his advanced age, adjust to the drastically changed diet.

The police guard who kept Tumanvow confined soon became aware of the great spirit that animated him, and became a Bahá'í himself. At night, the policeman would go to the villages and find people that he thought would be receptive, and brought them to Tumanvow to learn of the Faith. Soon there were a couple of people who declared their faith in Bahá'u'lláh.

On the night before the arrival of the boat to take Tumanvow home, he was desperate to find other souls to establish a Local Spiritual Assembly, as it was during the time of Riḍván. So he and the couple of new believers sat and prayed the Tablet of Aḥmad over and over for many hours. One by one people who heard that he was leaving in the morning came to see him one more time, and several declared their belief in this new Revelation. So they formed that night the first Spiritual Assembly of the Tokelau Islands of Samoa.

Tumanvow's loving-kindness towards his police guard had inspired that soul's heart to embrace the Faith and serve his community by assisting in the teaching of his people. Though suffering physical deprivation and physical stress from the drastic change in his diet on the new island, Tumanvow's three-month sojourn between boat travels was richly rewarded. His service to the Faith was recognized by the National Spiritual Assemblies of both Western Samoa and the British Isles, who were both responsible for the teaching work in that region of the Pacific Islands.[2]

'Abdu'l-Bahá has written:

> Think ye at all times of rendering some service to every member of the human race. Pay ye no heed to aversion and rejection, to disdain, hostility, injustice: act ye in the opposite way. Be ye sincerely kind, not in appearance only. Let each one of God's loved ones centre his attention on this: to be the Lord's mercy to man; to be the Lord's grace. Let him do some good to every person whose path he crosseth, and be of some benefit to him. Let him improve the character of each and all, and reorient the minds of men. In this way, the light of divine guidance will shine forth, and the blessings of God will cradle all mankind: for love is light, no matter in what abode it dwelleth; and hate is darkness, no matter where it may make its nest. O friends of God! That the hidden Mystery may stand revealed, and the secret essence of all things may be disclosed, strive ye to banish that darkness for ever and ever.[3]

To recognize the time in which we live, to understand the significance of this Day, to approach the life-giving waters of the Teachings for assistance, to memorize the Holy Texts, are all important steps we must take to transform our lives. However, it is in the field of action that confirmation and learning takes place. It is when we engage in service to humanity that we are tested in our faith and understanding and we continuously refine the apprehension of our true selves.

Shoghi Effendi says that we cannot comprehend the mystical, but we can apprehend or draw close to its fragrance and inhale its benefits. He writes of Bahá'u'lláh's Revelation: 'An exact and thorough comprehension of so vast a system, so sublime a revelation, so sacred a trust, is for obvious reasons beyond the reach and ken of our finite minds.'[4] It is in the field of action that our understanding grows, our reflection illuminates our understanding, and our refinement continues.

During the Ten Year Plan in the 1950s, pioneers left their homes to settle in the vast territories of the world to bring the Faith of Bahá'u'lláh and establish centres of light. It was in Johannesburg, South Africa that the light of the Faith found a resting place in the heart of Dorothy Senne.

Dorothy was a young woman when a small group of pioneers encountered her. The pioneers had struggled for nine months with no results or friendships made. It was dangerous and often illegal for whites to associate in any social way with blacks or coloureds in South Africa. However, the Guardian's instructions for the pioneers was to not teach the whites, but to concentrate their efforts on the black and coloured people of South Africa.

There was much hatred across the whole country and grave mistrust among the people. The pioneers struggled for these months to find someone whom they could trust to engage in a conversation about the Faith. As a small group of them were walking in Johannesburg, the local people looked upon them with mistrust and suspicion. However, when one of the pioneers came to one area, she noticed a young woman standing at her door with a bright and kindly face.

Dorothy Senne was only 22 years old and in her first year of marriage. She had an attractive and friendly demeanour, and a melodious voice. When the pioneer went back to the group, she mentioned that she had seen a woman whom she thought could be trusted, and they decided to return and bring her the Message of Bahá'u'lláh. When they returned, Dorothy embraced the Teachings almost immediately.

Not only did she embrace the Cause, but she arose to teach. She had strong organizational skills and began to organize meetings and gatherings. The Faith began to grow. Over the years, Dorothy served in many capacities and accompanied the youth to conferences in other countries nearby.

Her favourite topic was teaching and the Covenant, which she would teach at the Bahá'í summer schools. Her melodious voice would uplift all those who heard when she would recite the prayers of the Faith.

When Dorothy taught someone the Faith, she would tell them about where Bahá'u'lláh had written that if the Bahá'ís would not arise to spread the Word, God would raise up the stones. Dorothy carried a basket of stones with her when she taught, and after someone declared their faith she would tell them about this and give them a stone to remind them.

Dorothy was the first indigenous South African believer. Today the South African Bahá'í community is quite large and filled with the indigenous believers who carry on the work that Dorothy began.[5]

From these beginnings, small communities grew into larger communities. From the larger communities, the areas grew into active clusters. This organic process of change slowly and methodically transforms the hearts of people and begins to influence society. The Universal House of Justice, the world governing body of the Bahá'í Faith, tells us that

. . . involvement in the life of society should not be sought prematurely. It will proceed naturally as the friends in every cluster persevere in applying the provisions of the Plan through a process of action, reflection, consultation and study, and learn as a result. Involvement in the life of society will flourish as the capacity of the community to promote its own growth and to maintain its vitality is gradually raised. It will achieve coherence with efforts to expand and consolidate the community to the extent that it draws on elements of the conceptual framework which governs the current series of global Plans. And it will contribute to the movement of populations towards Bahá'u'lláh's vision of a prosperous and peaceful world civilization to the degree that it employs these elements creatively in new areas of learning.[6]

Lua Getsinger once told of an experience she had in 'Akká. She had made the pilgrimage to the prison-city to see 'Abdu'l-Bahá. One day He said to her that He was too busy that day to call upon a friend of His who was very poor and sick. He wished Lua to go in His place. He told her to take food to the sick man and care for him as He had been doing. Lua learned the address and immediately went to do as 'Abdu'l-Bahá had asked. She felt proud that 'Abdu'l-Bahá had trusted her with some of His own work.

But soon she returned to 'Abdu'l-Bahá in a state of excitement. 'Master,' she exclaimed, 'surely you cannot realize to what a terrible place you sent me. I almost fainted from the awful stench, the filthy rooms, the degrading condition of that man and his house. I fled lest I contract some terrible disease.'

Sadly and sternly 'Abdu'l-Bahá regarded her. If she wanted to serve God, He told her, she would have to serve her fellow man, because in every person she should see the image and likeness of God. Then He told her to go back to the man's house. If the house was dirty, she should clean it. If the man was dirty, she should bathe him. If he was hungry, she should feed him. He asked her not to come back until all this was done. 'Abdu'l-Bahá had done these things many times for this man, He said, and he told Lua that she should be able to do them once.[7]

This is how 'Abdu'l-Bahá taught Lua to serve her fellow man. And he writes:

O ye servants of the Sacred Threshold! The triumphant hosts of the Celestial Concourse, arrayed and marshalled in the Realms above, stand ready and expectant to assist and assure victory to that valiant horseman who with confidence spurs on his charger into the arena of service. Well is it with that fearless warrior, who armed with the power of true

Knowledge, hastens unto the field, disperses the armies of ignorance, and scatters the hosts of error, who holds aloft the Standard of Divine Guidance, and sounds the Clarion of Victory. By the righteousness of the Lord! He hath achieved a glorious triumph and obtained the true victory.[8]

Hand of the Cause of God William Sears used to say that the Concourse on High (those great souls who have passed into the next world) was waiting to assist us and all we had to do was 'poke a hole and duck!'

Our service to others and to society for the betterment of the world requires perseverance. It is not sufficient that we occasionally serve others. It must become a pattern of our lives. Service does not require a service project, a collective effort, or a distinct plan, although all those efforts are good to do. Service to others is a state of mind and a habitual intent followed by constant endeavour.

We must also listen carefully to the promptings of our hearts, as sometimes when we are quiet and meditating, instructions and suggestions come to us that are beneficial. The following story about India Haggarty was told by her sister Inez Greeven:

India Haggarty was a pioneer living in a hotel in Paris in 1931. This was 10 years after the passing of the Master, and 20 years after His visit to that city. There was another pioneer in Paris at that time, Mrs. S.

One night in 1931, India had a vision of 'Abdu'l-Bahá. He appeared to her and told her that He wanted her to go, right then, to her Bahá'í sister Mrs. S. 'Bring her flowers, and bring her money,' He said.

India got up out of bed and immediately prepared herself to leave her hotel. As she was fixing her hair in the mirror, her face was still radiant from the vision of the Master. She called down to the hotel clerk to summon a taxi for her.

She gathered up all of her money. She set aside the money

she needed for her personal expenses, and put all the rest of her cash into a small purse, went downstairs and asked the clerk, 'Where is the nearest florist shop?'

The clerk answered that there was one quite close by, but as it was just 5 a.m. it was certainly closed. India thanked him and waited for the taxi. When the taxi arrived, she requested that the taxi driver to please take her to that florist shop. The driver said, 'All right, but it's closed.'

She knew that the Master had a way for her to get flowers, and that he should take her there anyway. They arrived, and the windows were all dark. 'I told you it was closed,' the driver said. India said to take her to the next florist shop, and it, too, was closed.

As they drove through the city, they came upon the farmer's market area, where all the local growers brought in their vegetables and flowers to sell to the local stores. There was a wagon filled with flowers. India got out of the taxi and went over to the wagon with the flowers and asked the taxi driver to wait. She came back with an armful of red tulips, and got into the taxi. She handed the driver a slip of paper with the address of Mrs. S. on it, and they drove across Paris in the early morning darkness.

The taxi dropped India off at Mrs. S's front door, and she stood there, with her arms full of red tulips. She knocked at the door, heard a rustling, and the door opened. Mrs. S. was standing inside, wearing a heavy black coat, and it was obvious that she had been crying. Her face showed great distress.

Mrs. S looked at India, and at the red tulips, and cried out, 'OH! 'ABDU'L-BAHÁ!' and burst into tears. She sobbed and sobbed. She and India went into her home and sat down, and India tried to comfort her friend.

After she was composed, Mrs. S asked India, 'Why have you come here?' India answered that the Master had come to her in a vision, and that He had told her to bring flowers, and money. She handed the purse to Mrs. S.

Mrs. S. was astounded. When she could finally speak, she said, 'You think I am rich. Everyone does. And I did have money, but I ran out, and I was ashamed to tell anyone. There isn't one speck of food in this house. As you can tell, the house is cold; I cannot afford to heat it. I have been suffering, and I could no longer bear it. I decided, last night, to end my life. I awoke this morning, and I went and put on my coat. I decided to cast myself into the Seine and drown myself. I went to the front door, and was just putting my hand on the doorknob to go out, when suddenly, you knocked. I opened the door, and you were standing there. I could not believe my eyes.

Twenty years ago, 'Abdu'l-Bahá came to my house, in this city. And when I opened the door to receive Him, He was standing on my front porch – with an armful of red tulips. And to see you standing there with these tulips, and bringing this money, I could not believe it.'[9]

Shoghi Effendi comments on these inner promptings we sometimes experience, often as a result of dreams:

The purer and more free from prejudice and desire our hearts and minds become, the more likely is it that our dreams will convey reliable truth, but if we have strong prejudices, personal likings and aversions, bad feelings or evil motives, these will warp and distort any inspirational impression that comes to us . . . In many cases dreams have been the means of bringing people to the truth or of confirming them in the Faith. We must strive to become pure in heart and 'free from all save God'. Then our dreams as well as our waking thoughts will become pure and true. We should test impressions we get through dreams, visions or inspirations, by comparing them with the revealed Word and seeing whether they are in full harmony therewith.[10]

Further considerations

The purpose underlying the revelation of every heavenly Book, nay, of every divinely-revealed verse, is to endue all men with righteousness and understanding, so that peace and tranquillity may be firmly established amongst them. Whatsoever instilleth assurance into the hearts of men, whatsoever exalteth their station or promoteth their contentment, is acceptable in the sight of God. How lofty is the station which man, if he but choose to fulfil his high destiny, can attain! To what depths of degradation he can sink, depths which the meanest of creatures have never reached! Seize, O friends, the chance which this Day offereth you, and deprive not yourselves of the liberal effusions of His grace. I beseech God that He may graciously enable every one of you to adorn himself, in this blessed Day, with the ornament of pure and holy deeds. He, verily, doeth whatsoever He willeth.

Bahá'u'lláh[11]

Wherefore, be thankful to God, for having strengthened thee to aid His Cause, for having made the flowers of knowledge and understanding to spring forth in the garden of thine heart. Thus hath His grace encompassed thee, and encompassed the whole of creation. Beware, lest thou allow anything whatsoever to grieve thee. Rid thyself of all attachment to the vain allusions of men, and cast behind thy back the idle and subtle disputations of them that are veiled from God. Proclaim, then, that which the Most Great Spirit will inspire thee to utter in the service of the Cause of thy Lord, that thou mayest stir up the souls of all men and incline their hearts unto this most blessed and all-glorious Court . . .

Bahá'u'lláh[12]

Be thankful to God for having enabled you to recognize His Cause. Whoever has received this blessing must, prior to his acceptance, have performed some deed which, though he himself was unaware of its character, was ordained by God as a means whereby he has been guided to find and embrace the Truth . . . We cherish the hope that you, who have attained to this light, will exert your utmost to banish the darkness of superstition and unbelief from the midst of the people. May your deeds proclaim your faith and enable you to lead the erring into the paths of eternal salvation.

Bahá'u'lláh[13]

Remember not your own limitations; the help of God will come to you. Forget yourself. God's help will surely come!

When you call on the Mercy of God waiting to reinforce you, your strength will be tenfold.

Look at me: I am so feeble, yet I have had the strength given me to come amongst you: a poor servant of God, who has been enabled to give you this message! I shall not be with you long! One must never consider one's own feebleness, it is the strength of the Holy Spirit of Love, which gives the power to teach. The thought of our own weakness could only bring despair. We must look higher than all earthly thoughts; detach ourselves from every material idea, crave for the things of the spirit; fix our eyes on the everlasting bountiful Mercy of the Almighty, who will fill our souls with the gladness of joyful service to His command 'Love One Another'.

'Abdu'l-Bahá[14]

Exercises

1. Keep a journal of service to others and good deeds that you perform over the next two weeks. They can be as little as a kind word to a store clerk, or as much as a large project that you are involved in.

2. As you reflect on your journal, what have your learned? What went well? What needs improvement? In what ways would you change any of it?

3. What surprised you?

4. How might you increase the amount of service and good deeds in the next couple of weeks?

Conclusion

A rational proof for the immortality of the spirit is this, that no effect can be produced by a non-existent thing; that is, it is impossible that any effect should appear from absolute nothingness. For the effect of a thing is secondary to its existence, and that which is secondary is conditioned upon the existence of that which is primary. So from a non-existent sun no rays can shine; from a non-existent sea no waves can surge; from a non-existent cloud no rain can fall; from a non-existent tree no fruit can appear; from a non-existent man nothing can be manifested or produced. Therefore, so long as the effects of existence are visible, they prove that the author of that effect exists.

'Abdu'l-Bahá[1]

As the saying goes, we are spiritual beings having a physical experience. The awakening of the mind and heart to the association with our souls is our primary goal in this life. To feed and nurture the soul for its birth into the next world must be our constant endeavour – no one escapes that transition. The extent to which we endeavour to nurture our souls is reflected in the happiness that we achieve in this life.

Some questions that the soul yearns to investigate have been explored in this book. We began by exploring the nature of our 'first duty' to our Creator, to recognize His Manifestation. Understanding the significance of our creation and the time we our living in becomes the 'first obligation' we must pursue during the course of our lives.

Once we become aware of our true nature, we must endeavour to share with others what we learn and bring the knowledge of God to others as we fulfil the 'all-pervading concern' of our life. The success of our actions in teaching others depends on 'one thing' – that is to say, on whether or not the splendour of those principles we hold dear is visible to others.

Transformation is manifested positively when we practise the discipline of immersing ourselves in the ocean of the Holy Teachings, practise prayer and meditation, memorize the Holy Texts so we can share them in their pure form to others, and give service to humanity through goodly deeds.

In the early 1990s, I was working on a few projects at the Pentagon in Washington DC. I had the privilege of working at the Command level with the United States Air Force. The people I worked with were some of the most dedicated and trustworthy people I have known and have had the honour of working with.

After a gruelling week of work on a particularly difficult task, I travelled to Costa Rica on a teaching trip. When I got there, I was invited to accompany pioneer Alan Pringle, the husband of Counsellor Ruth Pringle, to travel to a few villages in the rain forest between San José and Limón. In each village we visited, the Bahá'ís greeted us with such joy and enthusiasm when they saw that it was Alan. Of course, I basked in the light while standing next to him.

In one area, we came to the foot of a mountain and had to walk to the top where a very dedicated family lived and farmed. On the property was a small house with no electricity or indoor plumbing. However, also on the property was a more modern building that had electricity and indoor plumbing. The owner of the property was so happy to show us the finally finished building that he had worked on for several years. 'It is for the gatherings of the youth and special meetings. Tonight, the friends will come from the area to listen to you,' he said with great enthusiasm. The electricity and indoor plumbing were used only at Bahá'í gatherings, not by him and his family.

The house that the family occupied was an immaculate mud-floor home for sleeping. The kitchen was outside with a tin roof attached to the house, covering the stove. We sat on tree stumps next to a large wide log used for the dining table and enjoyed a delightful and delicious lunch. While waiting for the lunch, the owner and I sat on the tree stumps and had a most enlightening talk. My broken Spanish sufficed and I was a bit in awe.

I had just come from a very sophisticated set of meetings with people who were some of the most influential geo-political strategists in America at the time. But the conversation with this man in the rain forest was world-embracing, as he easily quoted from the Writings of Bahá'u'lláh, commented on the discourses of Shoghi Effendi and enthusiastically wondered about the new messages from the Universal House of Justice. The talks at the Pentagon were earth-bound, while this conversation soared between earth and the worlds beyond.

That evening, the 'youth' building was filled with Bahá'ís from many villages in the area. Faces beamed as Alan, with his antique one-at-a-time slide projector, showed photographs from the Holy Land and various gatherings of Bahá'ís in Costa Rica. We sat long into the night before everyone left to walk the miles it took to get home. What a heavenly gathering! What a celestial gift I was privileged to partake in!

The next morning Alan and I travelled to Limón to visit the Bahá'ís in a small and impoverished suburb of that large port city. The people of Limón are Caribbean, speak mostly English and are of mostly African descent. They are very different from the rest of Costa Rica and live a relatively isolated life from the rest on the country.

When we walked up to a ranch-style home, Alan introduced me to one of the older believers in the community. My prejudice suggested an impoverished and probably a semi-literate man. He had a kind face and greeted us warmly. After a few greetings, the man turned to me and said, 'I have a few questions about the new Kitáb-i-Aqdas that maybe you can help me with.'

I replied that I would try, and he went into the house to get the book. This was shortly after the book had been released by the Universal House of Justice in 1992. We pulled up two folding chairs and sat in his garden while Alan went to visit some other Bahá'ís in the neighborhood.

'I am a bit confused about the structure of the book and do not fully understand how the notes and the references in the back of the book work. I seem to get a bit lost when going back and forth from the book's text to the numbered references and back again,' he said. I was speechless. I realized my prejudice, and was deeply embarrassed inside. I looked at him with new eyes.

'You know,' I said, 'I have been having the same problem. Why don't we sit here awhile and figure this out together?' And we did! What a glorious afternoon! What a wonderful lesson for me on learning humility!

We Bahá'ís have the great bounty of having 'Abdu'l-Bahá as our Perfect Exemplar of the Teachings of Bahá'u'lláh. We should often ask ourselves, 'If I was with 'Abdu'l-Bahá right now, what would I do? How would I act? What would He do?' As we struggle to put into practice what we learn in our lives we can visualize the example of 'Abdu'l-Bahá and attempt to emulate that example.

Throughout this book, we have mostly focused on what an individual must do to become a successful spiritual being. The Universal House of Justice reiterates numerous times the importance of the role of the individual, so clearly enunciated by Shoghi Effendi, in the successful unfoldment of Bahá'u'lláh's World Commonwealth.

In 1995, the House of Justice called upon the worldwide Bahá'í community to expand its activities to embrace all of the world's peoples in the development of a world spiritual enterprise. The core activities outlined by the House of

Justice provide a structured campaign to lift the conversations between the peoples of the world to the needs of the spirit; to engage in a devotional attitude towards the responsibilities of human beings to each other; to the stewardship of the planet and its environment both physically and socially; to teach each other about the spiritual realities that our Creator provides for us; to further the progress of an ever-advancing civilization; to ensure that all children have access to education both physical and spiritual; to prepare the youth of today to become enlightened leaders of tomorrow; and for each individual to engage in the process of the upliftment of each other and the betterment of the world.

Humanity is passing through the most difficult period in its chequered history. Organic growth, the obliteration of the old and the emergence of the new, depending on one's viewpoint, is either terrifying or filled with expectation – most likely both.

Shoghi Effendi has stated that World War II brought humanity to the outer fringes of the darkest period of its history. Without the spiritual armour necessary to awaken and nurture our souls, we will become victims of the vain imaginings and idle fancies of the darkness and negativity encircling humanity today.

The Bahá'ís, and especially the Bahá'í youth, must bring hope to a world that is falling further and further into the depths of despair and hopelessness. Here are Shoghi Effendi's prophetic words:

> The violent derangement of the world's equilibrium; the trembling that will seize the limbs of mankind; the radical transformation of human society; the rolling up of the present-day Order; the fundamental changes affecting the structure of government; the weakening of the pillars of religion; the rise of dictatorships; the spread of tyranny; the fall of monarchies; the decline of ecclesiastical institutions; the increase of anarchy and chaos; the extension and consolida-

tion of the Movement of the Left; the fanning into flame
of the smouldering fire of racial strife; the development of
infernal engines of war; the burning of cities; the contami-
nation of the atmosphere of the earth – these stand out as
the signs and portents that must either herald or accompany
the retributive calamity which, as decreed by Him Who is
the Judge and Redeemer of mankind, must, sooner or later,
afflict a society which, for the most part, and for over a century, has turned a deaf ear to the Voice of God's Messenger
in this day– a calamity which must purge the human race of
the dross of its age-long corruptions, and weld its compo-
nent parts into a firmly-knit world-embracing Fellowship – a
Fellowship destined, in the fullness of time, to be incorporated
in the framework, and to be galvanized by the spiritualizing
influences, of a mysteriously expanding, divinely appointed
Order, and to flower, in the course of future Dispensations,
into a Civilization, the like of which mankind has, at no
stage in its evolution, witnessed.[2]

We must all arise and, in the words of 'Abdu'l-Bahá, 'do battle
for His Cause in serried lines'! We must all follow the Words
of the Báb and mount our steeds of service, put on the armour
of our trust in God and, following 'Abdu'l-Bahá, bring hope
to the hopeless, strength to the weak, joy to the sorrowful and
vision to a world in darkness.

The field is indeed so immense, the period so critical, the
Cause so great, the workers so few, the time so short, the
privilege so priceless, that no follower of the Faith of
Bahá'u'lláh, worthy to bear His name, can afford a moment's
hesitation. That God-born Force, irresistible in its sweeping
power, incalculable in its potency, unpredictable in its course,
mysterious in its workings, and awe-inspiring in its manifestations – a Force which, as the Báb has written, 'vibrates
within the innermost being of all created things,' and which,

according to Bahá'u'lláh, has through its 'vibrating influ-ence,' 'upset the equilibrium of the world and revolutionized its ordered life' – such a Force, acting even as a two-edged sword, is, under our very eyes, sundering, on the one hand, the age-old ties which for centuries have held together the fabric of civilized society, and is unloosing, on the other, the bonds that still fetter the infant and as yet unemancipated Faith of Bahá'u'lláh.[3]

Bibliography

'Abdu'l-Bahá. *Japan Will Turn Ablaze!* Tokyo: Bahá'í Publishing Trust of Japan, rev. ed. 1992.

— *Paris Talks: Addresses given by 'Abdu'l-Bahá in 1911* (1912). London: Bahá'í Publishing Trust, 12th ed. 1995.

— *The Promulgation of Universal Peace: Talks Delivered by 'Abdu'l-Bahá During His Visit to the United States and Canada in 1912* (1922, 1925). Comp. H. MacNutt. Wilmette, IL: Bahá'í Publishing Trust, 2nd ed. 1982.

— *The Secret of Divine Civilization.* Trans. M. Gail. Wilmette, IL: Bahá'í Publishing Trust, 1957.

— *Selections from the Writings of 'Abdu'l-Bahá.* Comp. Research Department of the Universal House of Justice. Translated by a Committee at the Bahá'í World Centre and Marzieh Gail. Haifa: Bahá'í World Centre, 1978.

— *Some Answered Questions* (1908). Comp. and trans. Laura Clifford Barney. Haifa: Bahá'í World Centre, rev. ed. 2014.

— *Tablets of 'Abdu'l-Bahá* (etext in the Ocean search engine; originally published as *Tablets of Abdul-Baha Abbas.* 3 vols. Chicago: Bahá'í Publishing Society, 1909–1916). Wilmette, IL: National Spiritual Assembly of the Bahá'ís of the United States, 1980.

— *Tablets of the Divine Plan.* Wilmette, IL: Bahá'í Publishing Trust, rev. ed. 1977.

— *Tablets to Japan.* New York: Bahá'í Publishing Committee, 1928.

Bahá'í Education: A Compilation. Research Department of the Universal House of Justice. Wilmette, IL: Bahá'í Publishing Trust, 1977.

Bahá'í Institutions: A Compilation. New Delhi: Bahá'í Publishing Trust, 1973.

Bahá'í Prayers: A Selection of Prayers Revealed by Bahá'u'lláh, The Báb, and 'Abdu'l-Bahá. Wilmette, IL: Bahá'í Publishing Trust, rev. ed. 1991.

Bahá'u'lláh. *The Call of the Divine Beloved: Selected Mystical Works of Bahá'u'lláh.* Haifa: Bahá'í World Centre, 2018.

— *Epistle to the Son of the Wolf.* Trans. Shoghi Effendi. Wilmette, IL: Bahá'í Publishing Trust, rev. ed. 1988.

— *Gleanings from the Writings of Bahá'u'lláh.* Trans. Shoghi Effendi. Wilmette, IL: Bahá'í Publishing Trust, 2nd ed. 1976.

— *The Hidden Words of Bahá'u'lláh.* Trans. Shoghi Effendi. Wilmette, IL: Bahá'í Publishing Trust, 1970; New Delhi: Bahá'í Publishing Trust, 1987.

— *The Kitáb-i-Aqdas: The Most Holy Book.* Haifa: Bahá'í World Centre, 1992.

— *Kitáb-i-Íqán: The Book of Certitude.* Trans. Shoghi Effendi. Wilmette, IL: Bahá'í Publishing Trust, 2nd ed. 1950, 1981.

— *Prayers and Meditations by Bahá'u'lláh* (1938). Trans. Shoghi Effendi. Wilmette, IL: Bahá'í Publishing Trust, 1987.

— *Tablets of Bahá'u'lláh Revealed after the Kitáb-i-Aqdas.* Comp. Research Department of the Universal House of Justice. Haifa: Bahá'í World Centre, 1978.

Barrow, Reginald Grant. *Mother's Stories, and Stories of 'Abdu'l-Bahá as told by Muriel Ives Barrow Newhall.* Shawnigan Lake, BC: self-published, 1998. Available at: http://bahai-library.com/ives/stories/MSTORIES.PDF.

Calaprice, Alice (ed). *The New Quotable Einstein.* Princeton University Press, 2005.

Capra, Fritjof. *The Tao of Physics: An Exploration of the Parallels Between Modern Physics and Eastern Mysticism.* Shambala, 1975.

Colby Ives, Howard. *Portals to Freedom.* Oxford: George Ronald, 1943 and various reprints.

The Dawn-Breakers: Nabíl's Narrative of the Early Days of the Bahá'í Revelation. Trans. Shoghi Effendi. Wilmette, IL: Bahá'í Publishing Trust, 1932.

Honnold, Annamarie. *Vignettes from the Life of 'Abdu'l-Bahá.* Oxford: George Ronald, rev. ed. 1991.

Kaku, Michio. *Parallel Worlds: A Journey through Creation, Higher Dimensions, and the Future of the Cosmos.* New York: Anchor, 2004.

Leshner, Alan L. 'Science at the leading edge', in *Science*, 6 February 2004.

Lights of Guidance: A Bahá'í Reference File. Comp. Helen Hornby. New Delhi: Bahá'í Publishing Trust, 2nd rev. ed. 2004. Available at: http:// www.bahaistudies.net/compilations/hornby_lights_guidance.pdf.

Randall-Winckler, Bahiyyih. *William Henry Randall: Disciple of 'Abdu'l-Bahá.* With M. R. Garis. Oxford: OneWorld, 1996.

Ranjbar, Vahid Houston. 'The words of religion and the words of physics', online article at: https://bahaiteachings.org/words-religion -words-physics/.

Shoghi Effendi. *The Advent of Divine Justice* (1939). Wilmette, IL: Bahá'í Publishing Trust, pocket ed. 2006.

— *Arohanui: Letters from Shoghi Effendi to New Zealand.* Suva, Fiji: Bahá'í Publishing Trust, 1982.

— *Bahá'í Administration: Selected Messages 1922–1932.* Wilmette: Bahá'í Publishing Trust, 1980.

— *Citadel of Faith: Messages to America, 1947–1957.* Wilmette, IL: Bahá'í Publishing Trust, 1965.

— *This Decisive Hour.* Wilmette, IL: Bahá'í Publishing Trust, 1992.

— *Directives from the Guardian.* Comp. G. Garrida. New Delhi: Bahá'í Publishing Trust, 1973.

— *God Passes By* (1944). Wilmette, IL: Bahá'í Publishing Trust, rev. ed. 1974.

— *The Light of Divine Guidance: The Messages from the Guardian of the Bahá'í Faith to the Bahá'ís of Germany and Austria.* 2 vols. Hofheim-Langenhain: Bahá'í-Verlag, 1982, 1985.

— *Messages to the Bahá'í World, 1950–1957.* Wilmette, IL: Bahá'í Publishing Trust, 2nd ed. 1971.

— *The Promised Day Is Come* (1941). Wilmette, IL: Bahá'í Publishing Trust, rev. ed. 1980.

— *The World Order of Bahá'u'lláh: Selected Letters by Shoghi Effendi* (1938). Wilmette, IL: Bahá'í Publishing Trust, 2nd rev. ed. 1974.

The Universal House of Justice. *Framework for Action: Selected Messages* of the Universal House of Justice and Supplementary Materials 2006–2016. West Palm Beach, FL: Palabra Publications, 2017.

— *Messages from the Universal House of Justice 1963–1986: The Third Epoch of the Formative Age.* Comp. Geoffry W. Marks. Wilmette, IL: Bahá'í Publishing Trust, 1996.

Messages available online at https://www.bahai.org/library/:

— 'To the Bahá'ís of the World', Naw-Rúz 177 (2020). Haifa, Bahá'í World Centre, 2020.

— 'To the Bahá'ís of the World', The Riḍván Message, 153 B.E (1996). Haifa, Bahá'í World Centre, 1996.

— 'To the Bahá'ís of the World', The Riḍván Message, 155 B.E (1998). Haifa, Bahá'í World Centre, 1998.

— 'To the Bahá'ís of the World', The Riḍván Message 2010. Haifa, Bahá'í World Centre, 2010.

— 'To the Bahá'ís of the World', The Riḍván Message, 177 B. E. (2020). Haifa, Bahá'í World Centre, 2020.

Winger, Michael. *World Congress Tapes.* Produced for the Human Resources Task Force training the teams of volunteers at the Bahá'í World Congress, New York, 1992.

Notes and References

Foreword

1 Jason Neidrich is an inventor, scientist, microelectronics engineer, and author with publications in the fields of microelectronics, micro machines, and advanced semiconductor materials.

Introduction

1 The Universal House of Justice, Message to the Bahá'ís of the World, Naw-Rúz 177 (March 2020).

2 Shoghi Effendi, 'The goal of a new world order', in *The World Order of Bahá'u'lláh*, p. 35.

3 Letter from Shoghi Effendi, 5 July 1938, in *This Decisive Hour*, no. 41.

4 Bahá'u'lláh, *The Kitáb-i-Aqdas*, para. 181.

5 The Universal House of Justice, Message to the Bahá'ís of the World, Riḍván 177 (April 2020).

1. Accident or Creative Will?

1 'Abdu'l-Bahá, *Some Answered Questions*, no. 48, p. 219.

2 Ranjbar, 'The words of religion and the words of physics', on-line article at: https://bahaiteachings.org/words-religion-words-physics/.

3 Leshner, 'Science at the leading edge', in *Science*, 6 February 2004.

4 Bahá'u'lláh, *Gleanings from the Writings of Bahá'u'lláh*, XCIV, p. 192.

5 ibid. XCIII, p. 191.

6 'Abdu'l-Bahá, talk given in Washington DC, 23 April 1912, in *The Promulgation of Universal Peace*, p. 50.

2. The Created Spirit

1 Bahá'u'lláh, *The Kitáb-i-Aqdas*, para. 1, p. 19.

2   Kaku, *Parallel Worlds: A Journey through Creation, Higher Dimensions, and the Future of the Cosmos.*
3   'Abdu'l-Bahá, *Paris Talks*, no. 29, pp. 89–90.
4   'Abdu'l-Bahá, *Japan Will Turn Ablaze!*, p. 42.
5   Letter written on behalf of Shoghi Effendi to an individual, 12 December 1942, in *Lights of Guidance*, no. 1932.
6   Bahá'u'lláh, quoted in *The Dawn-Breakers*, p. 586.
7   Bahá'u'lláh, *Prayers and Meditations*, CLXXVIII, p. 299.

3. Purposeful Growth
1   Shoghi Effendi, *The World Order of Bahá'u'lláh*, p. 100.
2   Letter written on behalf of Shoghi Effendi to an individual, 18 February 1954, in *Lights of Guidance*, no. 391.
3   Shoghi Effendi, *This Decisive Hour*, p. 12.
4   'Abdu'l-Bahá, *Some Answered Questions*, no. 41, pp. 182–3.
5   Quoted by Bahá'u'lláh, *Kitáb-i-Íqán*, para. 267, p. 238.
6   Bahá'u'lláh, 'The Seven Valleys,' in Bahá'u'lláh, *The Call of the Divine Beloved*, p. 50.
7   Bahá'u'lláh, *Hidden Words*, Arabic no. 68.
8   'Abdu'l-Bahá, *Tablets of the Divine Plan*, no. 8. p.
9   The Universal House of Justice, Message to the Bahá'ís of the World, Riḍván 1966, in *Lights of Guidance*, no. 2011.
10 Shoghi Effendi, *The World Order of Bahá'u'lláh*, pp. 42–3.

4. The Act of Spirit
1   Shoghi Effendi, *The Advent of Divine Justice*, p. 44.
2   Letter from the Universal House of Justice to all National Spiritual Assemblies, 27 March 1978, in *Lights of Guidance*, no. 1097.
3   Shoghi Effendi, *The Advent of Divine Justice*, p. 43.
4   'Abdu'l-Bahá, *Selections from the Writings of 'Abdu'l-Bahá*, no. 34, p. 69.
5   Bahá'u'lláh, *Kitáb-i-Íqán*, para. 265, p. 236.
6   Bahá'u'lláh, *Tablets of Bahá'u'lláh Revealed after the Kitáb-i-Aqdas*, p. 196.
7   'Abdu'l-Bahá, *Selections from the Writings of 'Abdu'l-Bahá*, no. 209, pp. 264–5.
8   Letter from Shoghi Effendi to an individual, 13 May 1927, in *Arohanui*, no. 18, p. 28.
9   Letter on behalf of Shoghi Effendi to all National Spiritual Assemblies, 13 May 1955, in *Lights of Guidance*, no. 2036.

5. The Success of the Spiritual Enterprise

1 Letter from Shoghi Effendi to the Bahá'ís in the American continent, 24 September 1924, in Shoghi Effendi, *Bahá'í Administration*, p. 66.

2 Letter from Albert Einstein, 12 February 1950, quoted in Calaprice, *The New Quotable Einstein.*

3 Capra, *The Tao of Physics*, p. 137.

4 Drake Baer, writing in *Business Insider*, 2 June 2014.

5 The Universal House of Justice, Message to the Bahá'ís of the World, Riḍván 2008, in The Universal House of Justice, *Framework for Action*, pp. 62–3.

6 Shoghi Effendi, *The Advent of Divine Justice*, pp. 43–4.

7 Letter from Shoghi Effendi to the Bahá'ís of North America, 5 June 1947 (message known as 'The challenging requirements of the present hour'), in Shoghi Effendi, *Citadel of Faith*, p. 25.

8 Bahá'u'lláh, *Hidden Words*, Arabic no. 1.

6. One Creation, Two Worlds

1 Bahá'u'lláh, *Gleanings from the Writings of Bahá'u'lláh*, CXXXVI, p. 295.

2 ibid. CXXX, p. 285.

3 Honnold, *Vignettes from the Life of 'Abdu'l-Bahá*, pp. 163–4.

4 ibid. CXIII, p. 260.

5 ibid. XCIV, p. 193.

6 Shoghi Effendi, statement prepared for the United Nations Special Palestine Committee, 1947, also in Shoghi Effendi, Preface to *The Promised Day Is Come*, p. v.

7 Bahá'u'lláh, *Gleanings from the Writings of Bahá'u'lláh*, CLIII, p. 329.

7. Into the Light

1 'Abdu'l-Bahá, *Some Answered Questions*, no. 3, p. 9.

2 Shoghi Effendi, *The World Order of Bahá'u'lláh*, p. 195.

3 Bahá'u'lláh, *Epistle to the Son of the Wolf*, p. 26.

4 'Abdu'l-Bahá, *Some Answered Questions*, no. 61, pp. 261–2.

5 Bahá'u'lláh, *Gleanings from the Writings of Bahá'u'lláh*, CXXXII, p. 287.

6 Bahá'u'lláh, *Tablets of Bahá'u'lláh Revealed after the Kitáb-i-Aqdas*, p. 168.

7   'Abdu'l-Bahá, *Selections from the Writings of 'Abdu'l-Bahá*, no. 72, p. 110.
8   Bahá'u'lláh, *Hidden Words*, Arabic no. 63.
9   ibid. no. 33.
10 Bahá'u'lláh, *Tablets of Bahá'u'lláh Revealed after the Kitáb-i-Aqdas*, p. 173.
11 ibid. p. 168.

8. Breath of Life

1   Bahá'u'lláh, *Gleanings from the Writings of Bahá'u'lláh*, CXXII, p. 260.
2   'Abdu'l-Bahá, Tablet 'to the new friends of Korea', 5 November 1921, in *Tablets to Japan*, p. 15. Also in *Japan Will Turn Ablaze!*, p. 41.
3   Talk given on 26 November 1969, notes in Archives of the Bahá'ís of Nevada County, California, among the papers of Knight of Bahá'u'lláh Elise Schreiber Lynelle.
4   Shoghi Effendi, *Directives from the Guardian*, p. 86.
5   Quoted in Honnold, *Vignettes from the Life of 'Abdu'l-Bahá*, no. 27 in section 'His radiant heart', pp. 148–9.
6   As recounted to the author by Nili Moghaddam.
7   Bahá'u'lláh, Tablet translated from the Persian, in *Bahá'í Education*, no. 9, p. 3.
8   'Abdu'l-Bahá, *The Secret of Divine Civilization*, pp. 3–4.
9   'Abdu'l-Bahá, in *Bahá'í Prayers*, p. 103.
10 'Abdu'l-Bahá, *The Secret of Divine Civilization*, p. 109.

9. Water of Life

1   Bahá'u'lláh, *Tablets of Bahá'u'lláh Revealed after the Kitáb-i-Aqdas*, p. 200.
2   Bahá'u'lláh, *Gleanings from the Writings of Bahá'u'lláh*, CXXXVI, p. 295.
3   As recounted by Carole Allen, in Winger, *World Congress Tapes*, New York, 1992.
4   'Abdu'l-Bahá, quoted in a letter to Alfred E. Lunt in 1918, in *Star of the West*, vol. IX, no. 13, p. 141.
5   Barrow, *Mother's Stories*, p. 23.
6   'Abdu'l-Bahá, Tablet to Harry Randall, 17 September 1920, in Randall-Winckler, *William Henry Randall: Disciple of 'Abdu'l-Bahá*, p. 188.

7   Shoghi Effendi, *The Advent of Divine Justice*, para. 78, p. 78.
8   Another version of this story is found in Honnold, *Vignettes from the Life of 'Abdu'l-Bahá*, no. 126, p. 124.
9   'Abdu'l-Bahá, *Selections from the Writings of 'Abdu'l-Bahá*, no. 172, p. 202.
10 ibid. no. 115, p. 139.
11 'Abdu'l-Bahá, *Bahá'í Prayers*, p. 70.

10. Exercise of the Spiritual Being

1   Bahá'u'lláh, quoted in Shoghi Effendi, *The Advent of Divine Justice*, para. 39, pp. 36–7.
2   As recounted by Jack McCants, in Winger, *World Congress Tapes*, New York, 1992.
3   'Abdu'l-Bahá, *Selections from the Writings of 'Abdu'l-Bahá*, no. 1, p. 3.
4   Shoghi Effendi, 'The Dispensation of Bahá'u'lláh', in *The World Order of Bahá'u'lláh*, p. 100.
5   Recounted by Dorothy Senne's daughter, Tahirih Senne Linton, in Winger, *World Congress Tapes*, New York, 1992.
6   The Universal House of Justice, Message to the Bahá'ís of the World, Riḍván 2010.
7   Adapted from Colby Ives, *Portals to Freedom*, p. 85.
8   'Abdu'l-Bahá, *Selections from the Writings of 'Abdu'l-Bahá*, no. 208, p. 264.
9   As told by Inez Greeven, at her home in Carmel, California, around 1980.
10 Letter from Shoghi Effendi to an individual, 16 May 1925, in *Bahá'í Institutions*, p. 107; also in *Lights of Guidance*, no. 1739.
11 Bahá'u'lláh, *Gleanings from the Writings of Bahá'u'lláh*, CI, p. 206.
12 ibid. CXXXIX, p. 303.
13 Bahá'u'lláh, quoted in *The Dawn-Breakers*, p. 586.
14 'Abdu'l-Bahá, *Paris Talks*, no. 9, p. 29.
15 Bahá'u'lláh, *Hidden Words*, Arabic no. 1.

Conclusion

1   'Abdu'l-Bahá, *Some Answered Questions*, no. 60, p. 259.
2   Shoghi Effendi, last message to the Bahá'ís of the World, Riḍván 1957, in Shoghi Effendi, *Messages to the Bahá'í World*, p. 103.
3   Shoghi Effendi, *The Advent of Divine Justice*, para. 70, p. 70.

About the Author

Michael Winger's lifelong commitment to business innovation and diversity enabled his professional career to move from product innovation to organizational innovation in both the private and government sectors. His work in change management and strategic change brought him to advising senior management of Fortune 500 companies and senior leadership of the United States military, Department of Energy and other government agencies. Public speaking in his professional field has included, among many others, presentations at Carnegie-Mellon University on the integration of technology, business acumen and human dynamics; and on entrepreneurship at the *The Innovation Imperative* talks at the Universities of Oxford, Cambridge and London in the United Kingdom.

Michael has also served with various organizations that promote racial unity and the equality of women and men, including assistance in the development of strategic focus for NGOs on the status of women worldwide, for presentation to the United Nations General Assembly, as well as strategic consulting to the Tahirih Justice Center, an NGO that provides legal support to abused women seeking immigration status in the United States.

A dedication to the fostering of racial harmony and cultural diversity has taken him to over 45 countries, and to live in six, bringing the teachings of the Bahá'í Faith that foster the oneness of mankind and the development of a world consciousness.

In 2010, Michael retired from active business involvement and went pioneering for the Bahá'í Faith to Croatia where he currently resides.

Michael's previous books include *Friendship, Fellowship and Transformation,* published by George Ronald (2015); *Innovation Imperative: Your Future Depends on It* (2009), and *Journey of Ascent* (2014).

Ingram Content Group UK Ltd.
Milton Keynes UK
UKHW040709200323
418846UK00001B/223